GREAT MONTANA WEEKENDS

Fifty-Two Amazing (Fantastic, Unbelievable, Probably Pretty Good, Mostly Family-Friendly) Things To Do in the Big Sky State

Copyright © 2023 by Bangtail Press

ISBN 13: 978-0-9961560-7-3

Manufactured in the United States of America

All rights reserved. With the exception of short excerpts used for promotional, review, or academic purposes, no portion of this work may be reproduced or distributed in any print or electronic form without the written permission of the publisher.

Published in the United States by

Bangtail Press
P. O. Box 11262
Bozeman, MT 59719
www.bangtailpress.com

GREAT MONTANA WEEKENDS

Fifty-Two Amazing (Fantastic, Unbelievable, Probably Pretty Good, Mostly Family-Friendly) Things To Do in the Big Sky State

by Bangtail Press

DISCLAIMER

We've done our best to offer the latest information about Montana, but the state is going through a dynamic period of change. When it comes time to plan your trip, please don't take our word for it. This book is meant to be a starting place. Take a few minutes to do your own research before you leave the house.

If you find information in this book that is outdated, we would appreciate a heads up. Please email us:

bangtailpress@gmail.com

Karen Kenyon

TABLE OF CONTENTS

Introduction....11

SPRING

1. Fish a Tailwater.........18
2. Soak It!.........23
3. Snag a Paddlefish.........27
4. Hike the Ms.........30
5. Walk the Streets and Alleys of Butte.........33
6. Spend Ten Minutes of Silence on a Battlefield.........37
7. Help Out With a Branding.........40
8. Pick a Mushroom.........44
9. Hang Out in Great Falls During Western Art Week.........48
10. Hunt for Shed Antlers.........52
11. See Living History at the Bucking Horse Sale.........54
12. Sweep out a Shearing Shed.........56
13. Tip a Sunday Afternoon Drink.........58

SUMMER

14. Fish the Yellowstone River With a Guide.........64
15. Pan for Gold or Sapphires.........68
16. Listen to the Ghosts in Bannack.........70
17. Take an Artful Photo in Yellowstone or Glacier.........74
18. Visit Art in the Wind.........80
19. Climb a Peak.........85
20. Hike Underground.........88
21. Pick Some Flathead Cherries.........90
22. Go Car Camping.........92
23. Watch a Bird.........95
24. Follow a Dinosaur Trail.........98
25. Sing Along With the Anthem at a Rodeo.........101
26. Road Trip to a Music Festival.........104
27. Ride a Rented Horse.........108

28. Go for a Mountain Bike Ride.........110
29. Tube the Lower Madison or the Clark Fork.........112
30. Visit the Crow Fair.........115
31. Create a Menu from a Local Farmers' Market.........116
32. Whitewater Raft or Kayak.........118

FALL

33. Hear a Bull Elk Bugle.........124
34. Take a Jaw-Dropping Scenic Drive.........128
35. Work Montana's Stream Access Law.........131
36. Drop In on a Smaller Museum.........134
37. Paddle a Canoe Trail.........136
38. Bag Some State Parks.........139
39. Bend a Knee to Lewis and Clark.........144
40. Dip Into Essential Montana Books, Streamside.........148
41. Catch the Cat-Griz Football Game.........151
42. Bird Hunt on the American Prairie.........152

WINTER

43. Ski a Cross-Country Resort.........160
44. Cast and Blast on the Bighorn.........163
45. Hike Up the Bear Trap to Fish the Madison.........164
46. Fish Some Hard Water.........166
47. Check Out the Museum of the Rockies.........168
48. Visit the Montana Historical Society.........171
49. Ski a Mom-and-Pop Resort.........176
50. Ski a Closed Forest Service Road.........180
51. Rent a Snowmobile.........182
52. Fly Fish a Spring Creek.........184

Acknowledgments....188

INTRODUCTION

Home is a complicated notion. It's the place, as one writer put it, that you have to leave before you can know it for the first time. It's also the place, according to another writer, where, when you have to go there, they have to take you in. Home is sanctuary and surcease. When you step off a plane, it's the place that lets you draw an unguarded breath. It's the place where you go to tell stories about your travels. Here are the people, finally, who will receive your narrative—here are those for whom you've been traveling.

Home is also the place where, when you receive visitors, you are obliged to show them around. It's a responsibility canonized in pretty much any religion worth the name. When the wanderer appears at your door, you invite her in and offer her a meal, a bed. Hospitality.

Montana is our home. We've traveled a fair bit, and found no place that suits us better. And driving visitors around isn't a burden. We love to show off our home. Indeed, it's one of our favorite things to do—driving back and forth with friends and relatives, explaining where we live, offering a bit of history, a little context. This happens more often than you might think, and we're not alone in the number of visitors we receive. If you live in Montana and you have a guest room, chances are it's filled for a good portion of each summer.

But this impulse to share is also problematic, especially these days. It's qualified by the need to keep it to ourselves. So much of Montana, so much of the quality of life that we care about, depends on having privileged access. Fly-fishing with a friend on the Madison is so much better than fly-fishing elbow-to-elbow with a few hundred strangers. Day hiking to a waterfall with your dog is so much more enjoyable than hiking past pods of oblivious, iPhone-music-playing teenagers. And it doesn't even need to be said that skiing is best when you don't have to stand in a lift line.

So the problem in a nutshell: How do you follow that urge to share your home, that pull toward generosity, and yet retain the essential aspects of what drew you to the place to begin with? To put it another way: How much do you share? And how much do you keep to yourself?

MONTANA, WE'RE TOLD, is the Treasure State, it's the Big Sky State. We're the Last Best Place. We're also the hiking, climbing, camping, floating, fishing, bird hunting, big game hunting, downhill skiing, Nordic skiing, and take-a-few-photos-for-Instagram-while-you're-at-it state. For a start. We've never been short of recreational opportunities, photo ops, nor a complicated set of regional (geo) politics. *Oro y plata* (gold and silver) is on the state flag, but a better motto might be something like "Montana: Never Boring." In Latin, *Numquam taediosum*.

If you're in Montana, either visiting or digging in, it probably wasn't the economy that brought you here. More likely it was the lifestyle. Something about seizing the day and living in the moment. Finding yourself by leaving something behind. At times, maybe it feels a little overwhelming. With all there is to do, what do I do *today*?

To be a good citizen, and to be a part of the community, however, you also need to do more than *use* a place. You need to participate, to contribute. This means knowing a bit about the history and the social context, and how you might fit in. What are my obligations and what are my rights?

This book is intended to address both topics. What should I do with my time this weekend? And what's the context in which I'll be doing it?

And because we would be remiss if we gave anything especially cherished away, because it would feel like a betrayal, most of these suggestions are readily available to anyone with a smart phone and access to Google. Our intention is to offer a nudge here and there, hopefully urge folks to spend a few dollars at a worthy small business, maybe help out a struggling local taproom or horse outfitter.

> **Factoid**
>
> Montana is growing at a rate of about 1.6 percent a year. This is considered moderate growth. But the fastest growing Montana county, Flathead, is currently growing at a staggering 3.5 percent a year. Ravalli County and Gallatin County aren't far behind

Also, heads up that you're going to have to drive. Montana is a big state. We're a little over 147,000 square miles. Bigger than Germany. And if you were to drive from, say, the Dirty Shame Saloon in the Yaak to the Stoneville Saloon in Alzada (northwest corner to southeast corner), it would take you about 785 road miles and a little over twelve hours. It's hard to fully appreciate those distances until you're five or six hours into the drive. Point is, if you want to do something worthwhile this coming weekend, chances are pretty good you're going to have to burn some gasoline while you're at it.

Any attempt to understand Montana needs to begin with the geography. *Who* we are, in large part, is about *where* we are. The mountains, the plains; west of the divide, east of the divide; city, small town, ranch. Any generalizations about Montana must first acknowledge the significant regional differentials in character.

Montana has three very distinct geographical identities. There's Montana west of the divide, which tends toward higher precipitation, including Butte with its labor history and train wreck of a superfund site, as well as Missoula with the University of Montana and its ready-made arts community (lectures, readings, gallery openings) and stellar fishing on the Bitterroot. Elsewhere west of the divide, and to be objectionably reductive, Whitefish has tourism and moose sculptures, Big Mountain skiing and a Glacier Park tourist economy. There's extreme Northwest Montana with the Kootenai River and the tight hollers reminiscent of Appalachia (if you're in Montana for more than a week, you're bound to hear someone use that objectionable portmanteau, "Montucky"). And you can't forget Kalispell with its Flathead Lake influence (cherry festivals and art galleries).

East of the divide, you have Bozeman, which fifty years ago was an ag community heavily influenced by Montana State University but which is now, in addition to the thriving university (more than sixteen thousand students) a service economy for recreationalists and real estate buyers. The engines of this economy have become—not unlike Kalispell and Whitefish—tourism and development. Tyvek house wrap, nail guns, and a steady stream of contractor traffic between Bozeman and Big Sky. Long-time residents find themselves torn between resentment and gratitude.

When the commodity is solitude, it's hard not to begrudge the influx of those who would like to share it. But when the economy is driven by those same tourist dollars, and by the immigrant buying of homes and condos, it's also hard not to feel a certain amount of gratitude. It's a strange, vertiginous, disconcerting place to exist.

If you visit Montana, don't be surprised if most people are friendly but you also run into the occasional grump. Be sympathetic. Things are changing faster than most of us can absorb. And if you're already here, try not to be that guy. First come, first served works in restaurants but few other places. Unless you're Native American, you or your forebears came here from elsewhere. There's no reasonable rationale that would allow *you* to live here while shutting the door behind you. Behave accordingly.

Past Bozeman, there's the complicated, charming, thriving, dissolute, down-on-its-heels arts community of Livingston. The Yellowstone River runs through it, as does

The Murray Hotel and Bar in Livingston is famous for its history.

the railroad, and those two arteries inform pretty much every other aspect of life in town. Also, there's the wind. If you visit in the winter, don't be surprised if it's ten degrees warmer than Bozeman, but with sixty-mile-an-hour Chinook winds. Careful when you open your car door. It might get away from you.

Eastern Montana? It's the most under appreciated but, in so many ways, the most fascinating geography in Montana. The scenery doesn't knock you back on your heels like it does in the mountains but it's just as striking, just as beautiful. You might have to cultivate an eye to see it. The city of Billings, the largest municipality in the state, serves as a medical and shopping center for Northern Wyoming as well as Eastern Montana. If you live in Montana closer to Billings than Missoula, at some point you will likely have to visit a hospital in Billings.

The eastern part of the state—Bakken influence notwithstanding—has, by and large, seen a gradual population decline. The local economies tend to rely on agriculture, which is going through its own steady, lamentable transition from family businesses to industrial cogs in corporate gears. Make sure you've got a full tank of gas, your spare tire has plenty of air, and you have sandwich makings in the cooler. There are far, far fewer amenities in the east. Also, far fewer people. If you want to see what most of Montana looked like thirty years ago, spend time around Lewistown or Havre or Glasgow or Glendive.

As you spend your weekends in Montana, please be courteous, be mindful of the fact that this is always someone else's home, avoid talking politics, and most of all, be open and generous in your thinking.

Here's a funny thing: If you expect to have a good time, you almost certainly will.

SPRING

Spring is mud season in the Rockies, but it's also that time, after a long winter indoors, when we're all desperate to get outside. Therein lies a dilemma: balancing unpredictable weather against a need to get some air, some sunlight.

Recommendations for spring are biased toward this conundrum. Get outside! (When the weather permits.) And do something creative indoors! (When the storms blow through.)

There's also an odd sort of lethargy associated with spring, at least in our experience. Coming out the narrow end of a long winter, there's a vague suspicion that the light at the end of the tunnel could still be a train. Maybe it's better play it safe and stay in bed. Or perhaps just noodle around in the garden.

Nonsense. Go out to the driveway. Sit in your truck. Turn the key in the ignition. See what happens next…

1

FISH A TAILWATER

Tailwater fisheries offer some of the best—and certainly some of the most predictable—fishing in Montana. When all the other fisheries are blown out with spring runoff (roughly mid-April to mid-June) the tailwaters should be fishing just fine.

By "tailwaters" we mean those fisheries located just below a dam, as opposed to "freestone" or undammed, fisheries. For trout fishermen, the most famous Montana tailwaters are the Missouri below Holter Dam and the Bighorn below Yellowtail Dam. Both of these are "bottom draw" impoundments, which means that the water coming out of the dam has been released from the bottom of the lake. It keeps the water the same temperature, summer and winter, and creates a spring-creek environment for the fish. Insects hatch on a predictable cycle, and the fish never grow dormant with frigid water or sluggish with tepid flows. Libby Dam on the Kootenai and the Fort Peck Dam on the Missouri are also bottom-draw impoundments, though not quite so famous in terms of their fisheries. The Kootenai is big water, and best fished from a boat. Consider hiring a guide. The Fort Peck—improbably, given its Eastern Montana locale—supports a little-known (but apparently quite dynamic) trout fishery. We've never fished the Missouri below Fort Peck but it's on our list.

By contrast to these bottom draw impoundments, consider the Madison River below Ennis Lake. The Madison is rightly considered to be one of the best trout fisheries

Craig, Montana, a small town just a few miles below Holter Dam on the Missouri, is one of the unofficial epicenters of fly-fishing in Montana.

in Montana, but the lower Madison, below Ennis Dam, is primarily a winter fishery. Ennis Dam is a top-draw impoundment, which means the water coming out of the dam has already been pre-heated by the sun. Winters, you have a decent fishery, but in the heat of summer, the lower river is too hot for ideal trout habitat. It's best used by college students on inner tubes and rafts.

If you are a fly-fisherman, there are few better ways to spend a weekend in the spring (coming out of another long Montana winter) than by traveling to one of the tailwaters. The trout in these fisheries can be finicky, though. They see lots of flies floating past their noses. Given the abundance of food available to them and given the cyclic nature of their food supply (insect hatches can vary from hour to hour over the course of a day), they can afford to be picky. Even if you're not hiring a guide, drop into one of the local

Fishing the Missouri River from a driftboat, if your guide knows what they're doing, is the only way to fly.

fly shops and be honest about your inexperience. In exchange for dropping $50 or $100 bucks on some flies and tippet material, the shop should be happy to point you in the right direction.

Unless you live in Helena, Billings, or Kalispell, fishing one of the decent tailwaters might mean an overnighter. And since the weather's always iffy in the spring, think about ponying up for a motel. If you're fishing the Missouri, try to stay in Craig. Have a drink at Uncle Joe's Bar and eavesdrop on the guides in the corner, talking louder with each new round. Take note of the flies they're boasting about, and maybe pay attention to their complaints. Even the best guides will bitch about their worst clients. As a client yourself, therein lies a lesson or two.

If you're fishing the Fort Peck, be sure to drop in on the Fort Peck Interpretive Center. It's a top-shelf dino exhibit, and you'll likely have it mostly to yourself.

Kid Friendly

Watch out for cold, rainy weather. Bring hot chocolate and blankets for the kiddos. If you're hiring a guide, let them know you're more interested in having fun than catching fish. They'll plan accordingly.

FLY-FISHING ETIQUETTE

WITH MORE PEOPLE ON the water all the time, it's increasingly important to pay attention to the (mostly) unspoken codes of behavior agreed upon between experienced fishermen.

- As you put your boat in and out of the water, don't linger on the ramp. Get your boat ready before you back up, then push it off your trailer and get your vehicle out of the way as quickly as possible.
- When you float past a bank fisherman, give them room, well beyond the longest cast.
- If you're fishing on the bank, working your way up or down the river, don't jump past a fisherman to fish the next hole. Keep walking. Give them some room.
- Don't leave trash on the bank. This includes leader and tippet material.
- Release your fish (unless it's a whitefish for the smoker or a brookie for the pan).
- Be cheerful. Everyone on the water is there to have a good time. And nothing ruins a good time like bumping into a grumpy ass.
- If you hire a guide and a boat, the guide is the captain. He works for you but it's his boat. Behave accordingly.

All the above being said, you are still free to tell stretchers about the fish you almost caught and the flies you may have used. We're not uncivilized.

FLY-FISHING 101

IF YOU'D LIKE to try fly-fishing, the barriers to entry can seem intimidating. As opposed to spinner fishing, fly-fishing requires some basic training to even make a successful cast.

The casting actions are fundamentally different. Spin casting, the line is *pulled* out of the reel by the weight of the lure. Fly-fishing, the weight of the line *pushes* the thinner leader and attached fly forward. Keep your wrist stiff and pump the line. You're trying for a rolling loop that ends up setting the fly gently down onto the water.

Broadly, there are two types of fly-fishing. Dry fly-fishing means using a fly that sits on the surface. You're hoping a fish comes up from underneath to suck it down. The flies are meant to imitate winged adult insects. Wet fly-fishing, or nymphing, entails fishing under the surface, and using flies meant to imitate either minnows or the larval and pupal stages of insects. There are dozens of variations on these themes, however.

Fly-fishing is a bit like golfing. It's easy enough to buy some clubs and start swinging, but you'll be better off if you pony up for a lesson first. When you call your local fly shop to reserve a boat, be honest about your skill level. They'll match you with a guide who can give you a lesson or two.

2

SOAK IT!

The thing about Montana? What's happening above ground is only half the story. Below ground, there's an ongoing tale full of reversals and complications, a nail biter of fumaroles and burbling pipes and shifting tectonic plates. Yellowstone National Park, as most of us know by now, is actually a volcano that's due to blow somewhere around the time you finish reading this paragraph. Until it does, and lucky for us humans on the surface, it makes hot pots.

In a few, treasured places, Montana's groundwater gets heated up in the volcanic digestive track before being reintroduced to the surface at temperatures that lend themselves to self-indulgence. Writing this, it's hard not to go all chamber-of-commercey. When February segues to March, and you're twisted up with the mild depressions of winter, the best cure is a weekend pilgrimage to Chico in the Paradise Valley.

The amenity businesses built up around hot groundwater helps make the tail end of winter bearable. And the best

South of Livingston in Paradise Valley, Chico Hot Springs is one of Montana's more venerable institutions.

Fairmont Hot Springs, between Anaconda and Butte, has two large indoor pools and two large outdoor pools. As of this writing, you need to be either a hotel guest or a pool member in order to swim.

resorts have an infrastructure such that you can spend the day cross-country skiing or snowshoeing, maybe hire some sled dogs, and then kick back in the evening with a cold beer, squinting through the clouds of steam to see if you recognize anybody from your childhood.

Among the improved hot springs in the state, Chico Hot Springs, south of Livingston, is probably the best known. It's been around for more than a century, having been established in 1900. There was a fire some years back, and a building was replaced, but otherwise, many of the original structures remain. In addition to a pair of pools (a larger, warm pool and a smaller, hot pool), there's a well-historied saloon and a restaurant that'll knock your socks off. (Reserve weeks in advance.) If you decide to stay overnight, understand ahead of time that Chico isn't necessarily about pampering (although there is a spa). It's more about authenticity and local color.

Fairmont Hot Springs is a more traditional resort, and with larger pools. They have a golf course, tennis courts, and a small spa. And while there's a diner and a more formal restaurant, we've yet to have a really great meal there. And if you're on a romantic getaway for two, it may not be the first place to consider. It's a popular family destination, and the ratio of running and screaming kids to harried adults is about two to one. Either way, definitely pony up the extra few bucks for the outdoor water slide. Worth every penny.

Elkhorn Hot Springs in the Pioneers (south of Butte), Boulder Hot Springs (off the interstate between Helena and Butte), Norris Hot Springs (between Bozeman and Ennis), and Lolo Hot Springs (between Lolo and Idaho) are all more rustic variations on the theme. They're accessible during the day, but if you have kids in tow, be more cautious about after hours. The sun goes down, the partiers come out.

> **Factoid**
>
> *Chico Hot Springs was instrumental in a successful fight to save Paradise Valley and the Northern Yellowstone ecosystem from a gold mine. Go to* dontmineyellowstone.com *for more information.*

Bozeman Hot Springs, just south of Four Corners, used to be one of the more disreputable locations around, but now, after renovations, it's not only one of the largest public hot springs in Montana but also one of the most attractive. There are a couple of large indoor pools, some indoor hot tubs, and four large outside pools, along with a bandshell. It draws a large college crowd, so be cautious about late evenings if you have a family. There's also a gym attached, so you can pay a premium and get a workout before you soak. The lockers and showers aren't much to write home about, in our opinion, but they do the job. Heads up that they're closed on Saturdays.

Kid Friendly

Most every improved hot spring is perfect for kids during the day. Evenings, however, parents should be cautious about drinkers.

UNIMPROVED HOT SPRINGS

FOR THE MORE ADVENTUROUS, there are a handful of unimproved hot springs scattered around Montana. Most of them aren't especially convenient, which is kind of the point. The best of them need, at the very least, some sort of hike. Take a backpack with a towel and water bottles, beer in cans, maybe some sunscreen.

In Southwestern Montana, the Boiling River south of Gardiner used to be a very popular weekend getaway. Covid and the Yellowstone flood of 2022 threw a wrench into that one, though. As of this date, it's hard to tell when or if it might reopen.

Touring Hot Springs, Montana and Wyoming by Jeff Birkby is an excellent resource. That's probably your best place to start.

3

SNAG A PADDLEFISH

Montana's trout fishing grabs the headlines but for those in the know, few things are as compelling as a day spent snagging paddlefish.

Paddlefish are seventy-million-year-old (at least) living fossils that inhabit, within Montana, the Yellowstone and Missouri River watersheds. (There used to be a paddlefish species in China, but it's now almost certainly extinct.) Smooth-skinned and cartilaginous, they feed on zooplankton (filtering water through their overlarge mouths and gills), and so are impossible to catch with traditional lures. The oldest, largest specimens can push 150 pounds, the roe can pass for fine caviar, and the meat, if carefully prepared, tastes, in our opinion, like slightly oily halibut.

In the spring, during high water runoff, these compelling fish, pushed by the spawn, stack up at certain conspicuous locations. Pull into the fishing access at Fred Robinson Bridge on the Missouri River, or Intake Diversion Dam out of Glendive, and check out the rows of locals in chest waders, heaving out

If you're lucky enough to snag a big paddlefish, you'll be rewarded with stacks of excellent fillets in your freezer.

The Intake Diversion Dam, not far from Glendive, offers excellent paddlefishing—if you can catch it at the right time.

their surf-casting rods, tossing weighted treble hooks and then jerking them back in long, arduous pulls. They're hoping to snag a fish. It's not unusual to see forty, fifty, even a hundred fishermen lined up on the muddy banks. Once in a while, there will be a shout, then a run up the bank as the lucky fisherman follows his snagged trophy. It seems improbable until it happens. (A friend of ours, on first being exposed to paddlefishing, said it was like shooting across the river into the brush, hoping to hit a deer.)

These fish are tagged just like big game animals, and the tags are specific for the river. And each river, the Missouri and the Yellowstone, has its own set of regulations. On the Missouri, the season is open within a set window, while the Yellowstone closes when the FWP believes a harvest target has been reached. Seasons open in mid-May. Contact the Montana Fish, Wildlife and Parks the year before for tags.

If you don't have a tag, it might be worth a road trip just to watch the circus. Search social media and message boards to find out when the runs are peaking (usually late May). Bring a rod and reel and some bait, maybe some worms or bullheads, and fish for catfish while you watch the paddlefishers snag their dinosaurs.

Kid Friendly

Unless Mom and Dad are germaphobes, there are few things more enjoyable for most kids than splashing around on a muddy bank. The paddlefishing will be entirely beside the point. Bring a plastic spade and bucket, turn them loose, then plan on hosing them off when you get home.

PALLID STURGEON

ONE OF THE MOST ENDANGERED fish species in the world, the pallid sturgeon occupies much the same riverine habitat as the paddlefish. Unlike paddlefish, however, pallids are especially vulnerable to habitat disruption in the over-dammed Missouri. They have almost no new successful spawning recruitment in the wild. It has something to do with fingerlings being washed downstream and sinking to the bottom behind the dams. In that silt-heavy, oxygen-depleted environment, the fingerlings die.

There has been some success in breeding pallids in captivity and then releasing them back into their natural habitats, so it may be that the species isn't doomed. But they are still not reproducing in the wild. The jury, alas, is still out.

HIKE THE Ms

The American West has a long and somewhat puzzling tradition of displaying gigantic letters on hillsides. It goes back, apparently, to 1905 when U.C. Berkeley put a letter C above their campus. Fast-forward a few generations, and there are now roughly five hundred of these mountain monograms scattered around the West. Both of Montana's largest state universities—University of Montana in Missoula and Montana State in Bozeman—maintain their white Ms above town, and both have hikable trails leading up to them.

University Hall in Missoula opened in 1899, just six years after the university itself was established.

We like both. Hiking toward a destination adds an incentive, and once you reach the Ms, both have excellent views of their valleys. The trails can be crowded, but as long as you don't expect solitude, you should be fine.

In Bozeman, the M—made out of whitewashed rocks—was built in 1915 by MSU students. There is a parking lot just off the state highway at the mouth of Bridger Canyon, some distance away from the University. (It quickly fills up on nicer days.) Drive up toward Bridger Bowl, and the trailhead is on the left, well marked.

There are two routes to MSU's M. The more direct route is a straight-up grunt. We've done it a few times, and each time was the last time. The more civilized approach is a gentle, 1.6-mile gradient that switchbacks through varied terrain (open grass to timber) on its way to the M. The hike gains around 850 feet in elevation, and is punctuated by strategic benches.

> **HELPFUL TIP**
>
> *If you're hiking Montana's public trails with a pet, carry a little plastic poop bag in your back pocket. Keep an eye on your beloved animal and, when Fido stops to do his business, do the right thing...and pick up after your goddamned dog.*

In addition to serving as a great day hike location for most of us ten-pounds-over-weighters, MSU's M is also the finish line for the annual Ed Anacker Bridger Ridge Run. This is a bonkers extreme race that starts at Fairy Lake, heads up Sacajawea Peak, and traces the ridge line of the Bridgers for a total of 19.9 miles. Every year (Covid years excepted), 250 runners subject themselves to the 6,800 feet of elevation gain and the 9,500 feet of elevation loss that make up the race. Slots to participate are limited, and we understand it's quite competitive.

In Missoula, the M is just off campus. More convenient and more closely associated with the university than

Bozeman's M trail can be crowded, especially on a nice spring day.

MSU's letter, it's also less of a hike. The trail's about 3/4 of a mile to the top, zigzagging up eleven switchbacks across open hillside. You gain roughly 620 feet in elevation. It was first built in 1908, meaning that the Missoula students must have taken almost immediate inspiration from their Berkeley counterparts. The original whitewashed rocks were replaced with concrete in 1968.

You can continue on past the M for another mile to the top of Mount Sentinel. Take note as you go of the striations on the mountainsides around the valley. Those are watermarks from Glacial Lake Missoula, an ice impoundment that existed periodically between fifteen and thirteen thousand years ago. It was half the size of Lake Michigan, and played an outsized role in sculpting the geology of the Northwest.

Kid Friendly

Unless you're parent to some real troopers, most kids are going to spend at least a few hundred calories griping as they walk. But the hikes to the Ms offer a destination, and a final sense of accomplishment. Your kids will brag about how they made it to the top.

WALK THE STREETS AND ALLEYS OF BUTTE

The city of Butte is the closest city in Montana to heaven, if heaven is populated by hard rock miners, unionists, prostitutes, priests, housewives, transients, bartenders, drunks, tee-totalers, Irish and Poles, Czechs and Russians. At its peak, a century and more ago, there were as many as one hundred thousand residents in Butte, with most men laboring underground during the day and drinking hard at night. The history of Butte is one of labor struggles and kleptocrats controlling newspapers; it's a narrative of whorehouses connected by secret passageways and rock star socialists stirring up populist outrage before being lynched from bridges.

According to the Mining History Association, "By 1896 a five-square-mile section of the earth was producing 210,000,000 pounds of copper a year, over 26 percent of the world supply … and employing some 8,000 men with a payroll equivalent to $44,000,000 a month in

The history of Butte, as one writer has put it, is in effect the history of Montana.

Marcus Daly, one of Butte's "copper kings," stands at the entrance to Montana Tech, looking out over the city.

today's dollars…The by-product gold and silver amounted to some $500,000,000 a year, again at present-day value." I've read that enough copper was extracted from the area to pave a four-lane highway four inches thick, Butte to thirty miles past Salt Lake City.

Fast-forward more than a hundred years, and what's left is America's largest Superfund site, the Berkeley Pit. In 1955, certain mining operations segued from sinking shafts to excavating the surface. The pit operated until 1982. By the time it closed, nearly 1.5 billion tons of material had been taken out of the pit, including more than 290 million tons of copper ore. When operations were shut down, the water pumps were shut down as well. The groundwater immediately started filling the site. The pit is currently 7,000 feet long, 5,600 feet wide, and 1,600 feet deep. The water, at a depth of 900 feet, has an acidity roughly equivalent to lemon juice, and is laden with an array of toxic metals, including copper, arsenic, zinc, and cadmium. For a couple of dollars, from March until November, tourists can visit the Berkeley Pit viewing stand. It's worth it.

They have recently begun treating the water to avoid spillover, processing it at roughly the same pace as it's rising. But if this toxic pool is ever allowed to spill out into nearby Silver Bow Creek, it will then flow into the Clark Fork River. Which of course flows into the Columbia.

Among the things to see and do in Butte, there's an enormous statue of Mary overlooking the city, lit at night. You can pay for a bus tour if you're of a religious mindset. And then there's the annual Montana Folk Festival. Most of the events are free, and some of the performers are world class. And don't forget the annual booze-a-palooza of Saint Patty's day, complete with parade and city-wide stagger, bar to bar. (In our fifties now, we're not sure you could pay us enough to hit Butte on March 17. But some folks seem to like it.)

Walkerville, a Butte community at the top of the hill, offers a glimpse of history through its ghost signs.

Butte is also one of America's great walking cities. Seriously. If you find yourself driving through between Missoula and Bozeman, take a few hours on a slow weekday and simply walk the streets. You are now passing through America's largest National Historic Landmark district, with more than six thousand registered buildings. Check out the Copper King Mansion on West Granite. This thirty-four room house was built in 1888 by William Andrews Clark, in his day one of the wealthiest men in the world. It's operated as a B&B now. Stay there, if you can. Maybe go to the Dumas Brothel Museum, built in 1890 and still operating as a brothel as late as 1982. Consider the "ghost signs" that are still visible on the brick sides of a number of buildings. These are advertisements for products that have long since gone the way of the dodo, but the promotions remain. Find the interactive exhibit, overlooking town, for the 1917 Speculator Mine disaster—168 men were killed. It's still the deadliest hard rock mining catastrophe in American history.

There's something to be said for a free-form meander up and back, particularly if you have a good reference book or two in your pocket. But you should also consider hiring a guide. Perhaps look into "Old Butte Historical Adventures."

> **Factoid**
>
> *At one point, there were thirty-eight different nationalities living and working in Butte. The city was so diverse that the "No Smoking" signs posted in the mines had to be printed in fourteen different languages.*

Kid Friendly

Understandably enough, most kids aren't going to be interested in what happened before they arrived on the scene. As incentive, maybe promise them a swim at Fairmont after you're done.

6

SPEND TEN MINUTES OF SILENCE ON A BATTLEFIELD

A character in one of William Faulkner's novels says, "The past isn't dead and buried. In fact, it isn't even past."

Here in Montana, our history is still pretty fresh. It's so fresh, in fact, that it's not even really history. Most of our major events took place only four or five generations ago. It's only been a little over two hundred years since John Colter ran through his gauntlet of Blackfeet at the Three Forks of the Missouri. The grandparents of those still alive today could have easily participated in the famous union strikes of Butte in the early 1900s. And the significant battlefields of Montana, despite how they may seem at first glance, despite the institutional veneer of distance, are all fresh enough to sting.

A bit of advice? Not unlike preparing for a trip to the museum, before you take the time and effort to visit a battlefield, spend a few days brushing up on

A memorial at the Bear Paw Battlefield commemorates Chief Joseph's surrender speech.

Montana Weekends 37

Nez Perce Chief Joseph surrendered to Nelson Miles after a flight of almost 1,200 miles.

your reading. If you're going to the Bear Paw Battlefield south of Chinook, or the Big Hole Battlefield south of Butte, bring yourself up to speed on the flight of the Nez Perce. We recommend starting with *Chief Joseph & the Flight of the Nez Perce: The Untold Story of an American Tragedy*, by Kent Nerburn. That one's pretty good. And if you're visiting the Little Bighorn, we recommend Nathan Philbrick's *The Last Stand*, one of the more entertaining (if not necessarily the most exhaustive) looks at Custer and Sitting Bull.

One more recommendation: Once you're on the battlefield itself, finagle some time alone. Find a few feet of grass away from everyone else. Sit down. Close your eyes. Imagine the sound of rifle shots, hear the scream of horses, feel the dryness in your mouth in anticipation of the coming fight. Recreate fear at the distinct possibility that you might die within the next few minutes. There are villains in these stories, and there are heroes, but we all have in common the fact of our biology. We're all human beings here. Consider the scorn of soldiers, biased by the racism of the day. The concern for the good opinion of your fellow soldiers. The fear that you might be seen as a coward.

Lakota Chief Sitting Bull helped defeat George Amstrong Custer.

Consider the vertigo and despair of the Indians at seeing their lives overturned. The grief at seeing their homelands stripped away, their family members murdered. Consider this landscape of wind and grass and bones torn apart by hatred and intolerance, heroism and sacrifice, atrocity and bloodshed.

And now there's you. The decision to tour a battlefield might have been made flippantly, maybe at the last minute. "Might as well go take a look." But now you are here to stand witness. However inadvertently, you have become part of the story as well.

If you're touring the Battle of the Little Bighorn during tourist season, consider booking a couple of hours with Apsáalooke Tours. Your guides will likely be Crow Indian, and will offer an essential perspective. If you're considering the Bear Paw Battlefield, stop in at the Blaine County Museum in Chinook first. They have a top-shelf exhibit.

Kid Friendly

Battlefields are history made manifest. If you've done a little bit of homework, maybe you can talk to your kids about troop movements and personalities, use the landscape to illustrate who did what and why.

Great Montana Weekends 39

7

HELP OUT WITH A BRANDING

Here's Montana Ranching, 101: Working ranches in the West are producers of marketable commodities. Driving past on the interstate, when you see cows and calves grazing behind fences, you're seeing an asset literally growing, gaining weight. When those calves are sold in the fall, the price they bring will be in large part determined by how much they weigh. Every other visible aspect of the ranch—the stacks of hay for feeding in the winter, the tractors for tending the hay ground, the corrals, the horses, the water tanks—it's all designed to more efficiently produce and monetize beef.

Most cattle ranches are cow-calf spreads, with a small herd of bulls on the side. This means that a herd of mother cows is maintained year-round—bred in the fall, calving in the spring—with a certain number of "dry" (or unimpregnated) cows sold off every year, along with that year's calves. The cows and calves (bulls are kept in separate pastures), from calving in the spring until shipping in the fall, are left out in the open pasture, living a pretty good life, all

Traditional branding methods typically require several hands to hold the calf.

things considered. As opposed to most of the beef raised in the United States, Montana cattle have the advantage of fenced range. They have lots of room to play. When they're shipped in the fall, they're typically shipped to feedlots, which adds another layer of moral complexity to the beef you eat. But prior to shipping, the cattle in Montana... you'd have to say they're living the high life.

Raising cattle is, by necessity, often a communal effort. You can never go it entirely alone. Neighbors help each other out. To take only one example, when a fence is shared between property owners, the upkeep of that fence is split. I'm responsible for the left hand half of my fence, while you're responsible for your left hand half. It's taken for granted that each landowner will do his or her part. If you drop the ball in this regard, there's no end to the derision and scorn that will be politely and tactfully heaped on you behind your back. Among the many communal ranching efforts you'll see in a given year, brandings are one of the

A good cow horse will know when to help pull a rope taut and when to let it go slack.

most important. If you're ever given an invitation to attend a branding, you need to go. Just go.

First thing in the morning on branding day, the mother cows with their new calves are rounded up, then separated. The calves get their own corral. If the ranch chooses to do things the old-fashioned way, you'll see horses and lariats, maybe some cow dogs pushing cows one way, calves the other. After the calves are separated (the cows will be making a cacophony of moos, calling to their calves) each calf is then either roped ("heeled") and tossed to the dirt (old-fashioned way) or herded into a chute and trapped in a metal calf table. Once the calf is prone and restrained (either under knees and with ropes, or pressed between metal grills), a hot branding iron is applied to a portion of the calf. Each brand is registered and unique to the ranch. The placement of the brand is part of the registration—right ribs, left hip, right shoulder, etc. Branding will take about three seconds, and may be accompanied by a flash-fire of hair. When the hair grows back, it will be in a different color and pattern.

> **Factoid**
>
> *The practice of branding livestock goes back to at least 2,700 BC. An Egyptian tomb painting depicts cattle being branded. Today, branding is still the most practical way of identifying cattle ownership.*

In addition to the branding, the calves are inoculated, trimmed of their horns, and the bull calves are nutted (castrated). The testicles are tossed in a bucket, either to be deep fried later as Rocky Mountain oysters or, at the very least, used as theatre props to tease the newest members of the branding party. A bloody hand will invariably hold up three or four in an open palm. "You hungry?"

Branding chutes and calf tables have taken some of the load off spring brandings. The work isn't nearly as labor-intensive as it used to be. Nevertheless, it's still a communal effort, and afterwards, there will be some sort of shared meal. Burgers and brats, casseroles, salads, beers and sodas pulled out of icy coolers, and most of all, the camaraderie and satisfactions of shared labor. The cows and calves, reunited, will graze peacefully just outside the fence, the trauma of the branding already forgotten.

Kid Friendly

Ranching is a family affair. The kids helping out on a ranch aren't children, as one writer put it, but rather men and women in training. Put 'em under a cowboy hat and find a pair of boots that kind of fit, set them on your lap while you hold a calf's hind leg.

BRAND IDENTITY

THERE ARE CURRENTLY MORE than 55,000 registered brands in the state of Montana. The only state with more is Texas. And while you can register new brands, they have to follow a strict set of guidelines. They can only be letters and numbers, with a limited set of other shapes and characters (bar, slash, box, diamond, etc.) If you have an older brand, something that uses shapes instead of letters, you might own a valuable asset. There's a funny little commodities market around older brands. Especially if there's some history behind them, old brands can be quite valuable. Ranchers will sometimes pay thousands of dollars for a really good one.

8

PICK A MUSHROOM

It is with enormous regret that we need to report an insidious, pervasive conspiracy in the state of Montana. There is an underground cabal of sadistic, like-minded mushroom enthusiasts who fervently maintain that it's possible to simply go out in the woods in the spring and somehow find morel mushrooms. These are superb actors, all of them, never once cracking a smile or admitting to the joke. Collectively, they have made life marginally more difficult for those of us who aren't in the club. They also clearly have some sort of connection in the mountains of Oregon or maybe Washington wherein they can get buckets of morels shipped to them overnight to freeze or dehydrate and haul out at strategic times. "Check out what I found up Rock Creek. You like morels?"

To judge by social media posts, those of us who know better—who have spent hours, days, in the woods, fruitlessly searching for the tiny little Easter eggs of fungal goodness only to come home empty-handed, tired, blistered, frustrated—are distinctly in the minority. We're a dwindling crowd, us the skunked mushroomers, but you can still find us on Saturday evenings in most of the mountain dive bars in Montana. Sweat-stained and dirty

Montana has a bounty to offer those who know how to harvest it. Exhibit A: morel mushrooms.

nailed, nursing our beers with resentment and bemusement. Is it our fault that we can't find morels?

Yes. Yes it is.

There's a knack to finding morels, and we don't have it. But if you manage to click into that particular groove, there are few more productive and enjoyable ways to spend a Saturday afternoon in late April or May in Montana. Not unlike picking hucks in the late summer, going after morels in the spring adds a nice sense of purpose, if you need it, to a walk in the woods. For kids, if they can click into the groove as well, it becomes an especially tasty kind of Easter egg hunt. And again, not unlike berry picking, mushroom hunting offers a nice little life lesson about the world outside the back door. Food doesn't come from the grocery store, after all. It comes from the ground. Pay attention.

There is also a subculture of mushroom pickers out there, and they take themselves quite seriously. There's a lot of money to be made if you're good at it and the season's productive. A pound of dried morels, as of this writing, can go for more than $150. Don't be surprised if you run into the occasional commando-style picker, overzealous and protective of his or her secret spots. That's fine. Just pivot and head in the opposite direction.

> **HELPFUL TIP**
>
> Almost 30 percent of Montana is public lands, whether BLM, National Forest, or state lands. But that also means that 70 percent of Montana is restricted. It's important to know where you are at any given time. A phone app that's marketed to hunters, onX, will show you property types and boundaries.

We're told that this year's morels prefer last year's burnt timber. When you're thinking about where to go, maybe pay attention to where last year's forest fires were, and then start there. Look for them in the moist soil and shaded areas beside logs. You can also find them, we're told, on riverbanks. They're only a couple of inches tall, and they're often the color of the ground, so they're easy to miss, pushing up out of the bracken. If you do find a few, use a knife to cut at their stems rather than pulling them out of the ground. Note the area. Put it into your GPS. You'll probably find them there again next year.

Spread your stash out on the ground and take a picture, post it to social media. Remember that everyone who congratulates you so graciously is secretly gnashing their teeth.

Kid Friendly

Morels often can be bought, in season, at a local farmer's market. You might want to buy a few and fry them up for breakfast. When your kids decide they love them, suggest a morel expedition into the mountains. It might be all the incentive they need.

INVASIVE SPECIES

Some of the most severe and ongoing threats to the ecology of the West are species of non-native plants, insects, animals, and mollusks that evolved elsewhere and were then introduced to this new environment. In their native habitats, appropriate and natural controls co-evolved with them. As the species have been displaced to their new environments, however, those controls are either absent or less effective, allowing for explosive growth—to the detriment of native species.

There are places in Montana, particularly west of the divide, where, in late summer, you'll see entire hillsides carpeted with a pleasant purple bloom. This is spotted knapweed (detail at bottom), and it's an ecological catastrophe. Mostly inedible by native grazers (elk, deer, etc.), knapweed also outcompetes almost every other plant in the ecosystem. Uncontrolled, it can take over a habitat. Those purple hillsides are the botanical equivalent of Chernobyl.

Other introduced plant species in Montana include leafy spurge (inset photo), Dalmatian toadflax, and saltcedar, among many others.

If you're hauling a boat through Montana, prepare to be stopped at various checkpoints. These are zebra mussel check stations. Montana is trying to keep this aggressive invasive out of our rivers and lakes.

9

HANG OUT IN GREAT FALLS DURING WESTERN ART WEEK

If Montana has a patron saint, it's got to be Charles M. Russell.

Cowboy artist "Kid" Russell first visited Montana at the age of sixteen, and came again to stay for good a couple of years later, in 1882. A brilliant artist, he was also authentic cowboy, boot heels to brim. His art was always informed by his own exceptional experiences. During his lifetime, he produced some 4,000 pieces—paintings, drawings, illustrated letters, sculptures—including the mural, *Lewis and Clark Meeting the Flatheads at Ross' Hole*, which hangs in the Montana State Capitol.

The C. M. Russell Museum in Great Falls houses a good portion of Russell's work. Every year since 1969 (Covid delays excepted), around the time of Charlie's birthday on March 19, the museum has held a fundraising auction event called "The Russell." Since the first auction in 1969, a larger complex of events and displays, collectively called Western Art Week, has grown up around the event.

"The Russell" is the annual fundraising auction and show sponsored by the C. M. Russell Museum.

A reception for the "The Russell," above, and the master himself, Charlie Russell.

During this one week in March, the city of Great Falls is filled with some of America's top Western and wildlife artists. More than eight hundred artists roll into town to set up shop in hotel rooms and booths, hang canvases and lug bronzes from tailgate to pedestal, arrange jewelry in display cases and position guest books for signature. The Heritage Inn alone, on the west side of town, hosts over two hundred artists. Think bolo ties and cowboy boots, spotless Stetsons and *hors d'oeuvres* passed around on trays.

There's also a certain kind of hierarchy in place. Those artists who have been juried into the auction itself hold a privileged spot, while the remainder (and vast majority) of the artists are, in our opinion, treated rather like second-class citizens.

As you browse and rotate through, painting to painting, room to room, you will occasionally be told what you should pay most attention to, what you should appreciate.

There were originally five "great falls" on the Missouri River. The four remaining, while diminished by dams, are still impressive.

Keep in mind: At the end of the day, the gas in the engine of the art world is money. If your work sells, respect follows. If the market, obeying the push and pull of its own arcane tidal charts, elects not to pay attention (no matter your accomplishments on the canvas), you're going to find yourself beached and becalmed in a corner off by yourself.

When we've attended Art Week, we've always found it a little disconcerting to see all these exceptionally talented artists, lined up one after the other, waiting for attention. It's an outstanding opportunity for potential collectors, having so much art crammed into one place, but it is also a diminishment of the artists themselves. A lifetime spent honing your talent only so you can stand in the door of a hotel room, smile pasted on, waiting for a bank president to drop in and haul out his checkbook.

> "In my book a pioneer is a man who turned all the grass upside down, strung bob-wire over the dust that was left, poisoned the water, cut down the trees, killed the Indian who owned the land, and called it progress. If I had my way, the land would be like God made it, and none of you sons of bitches would be here at all."
> —Charlie Russell

Or maybe that's cynicism. Everybody's a willing participant, and for most of us casual enthusiasts, the budget-minded aesthetes, there's no better time or place to get an introduction to the current state of art in the West.

While you're in Great Falls, drop in on the Sip 'n Dip Lounge in the O'Haire Motor Inn. The back bar is a window into the swimming pool. They'll occasionally dress up some pretty girls in mermaid costumes and ask them to swim around. This is camp elevated to art.

The city is also quite proud of its skate park (the largest in the state, we're told), and Giant Springs State Park, with associated walking trails, is worth an afternoon, at least. Pack a picnic.

Check out visitgreatfallsmontana.org for Art Week dates, a schedule of events, and other essential information.

Kid Friendly

Western art might not be of interest to kids, but Great Falls has a children's museum that's worth a visit. Kids will also enjoy Giant Springs State Park fish hatchery where they can feed the trout. Teenagers with a board will dig the skate park.

MALMSTROM AIR FORCE BASE

EVERY CITY IN MONTANA maintains a certain kind of essential character that's been informed by its economy. There are mining towns, ag towns, tourist towns...Great Falls is a military town, influenced by Malmstrom Air Force Base, an installation just east of the city. Established during WWII, Malmstrom is currently home to 3,146 active service members, 3,137 family members, 619 civilian employees, and more than 800 contractors.

10

HUNT FOR SHED ANTLERS

Among the more valuable commodities produced by Montana (wheat, barley, beef, wool, beets), you wouldn't think to list antlers. And yet, as of this writing, Grade A elk antlers are going for around $14 per pound. Given that a big antler might weigh 35 or 40 pounds...well. It ain't chopped liver.

Bull elk typically shed their antlers in March and early April. If you're interested in looking for some bone (as the enthusiasts call it), scout it out ahead of time. Drive some back roads, scope some open hillsides. If you spot bull elk on public land in February, you might find their antlers in the same spot in April.

The Sun River Wildlife Management Area, wintering grounds for a large elk herd, opens May 15 to the public. We haven't been to this particular circus, but have heard it's quite a scene. Hundreds of bone hunters on horseback and in trucks, racing to be the first to pick up the obvious antlers. Sounds like something to watch from a distance.

Kid Friendly

Timing is everything in shed hunting. Go too early and you'll find yourself postholing through snow drifts. Go too late, you'll miss the low-hanging fruit. Shoot for mid-April (after checking for any seasonal closures) and make sure your kids have good boots.

SEE LIVING HISTORY AT THE BUCKING HORSE SALE

There are a few famous (and infamous) city-wide parties in Montana. There's Butte on Saint Patty's day, Livingston over the Fourth of July, and Miles City during the Bucking Horse Sale.

Held during the third full weekend in May, it's a three-day event (four, if you count the opening night concert), and while the backbone of the party is still, as it has been since 1951, contractors showing off their rough stock to potential buyers, there are a bunch of other events as well, many of which harken back to the days of old fashion ranch rodeos. It's hard to find a good mutton bustin' or sheep shearing competition these days, not to mention a wild horse race, but Miles City usually comes through. There are also other, less traditional events that have attached themselves to the weekend. An artist's quick draw competition and some vendor booths at the fairgrounds come to mind.

Kids and families will be most interested in the rough stock rodeo, and a wild horse race makes for good entertainment no matter how old you are. But the Friday and Saturday

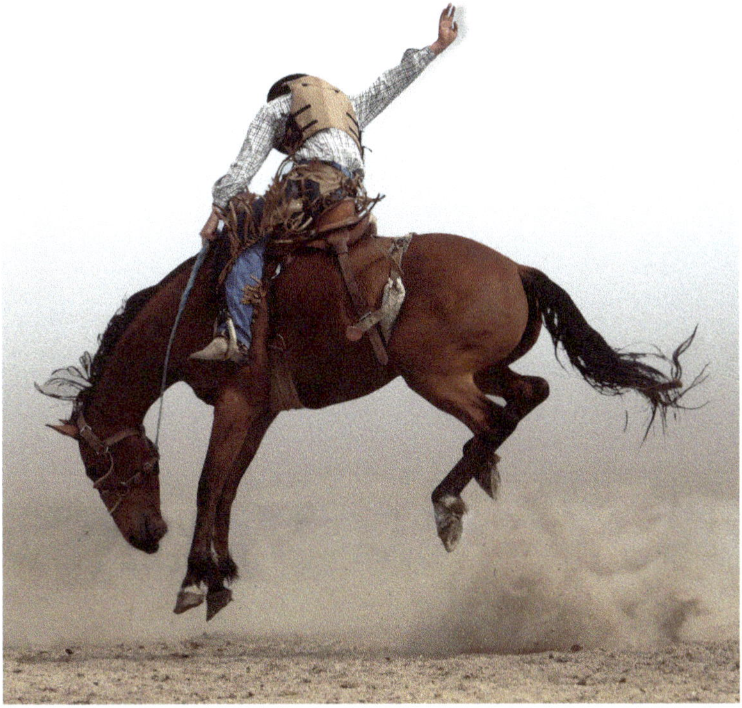

Margo Harrison / shuttserstock.com

Some horses buck better than others. An eight-second ride can determine the career not only of the rider but of the roughstock as well.

night street parties are for the grownups. The Montana Bar on Main Street has been around since 1908, and is one of the informal hinges of the weekend. For our money, we'd rather hang out in a bar that's not jam-packed wall to wall, but if you like the bar scene, you should probably experience it at least once.

Miles City is, in many ways, the heart of Montana's cowboy culture. While you're in town, drop in on the Range Riders Museum. It will give you a sense for the essential role cowboying played in our history.

Kid Friendly ☆☆☆☆☆

The Bucking Horse Sale is a party, start to finish. Pick your events to make sure the kid-friendly party doesn't overlap with the adult-sized portions.

12

SWEEP OUT A SHEARING SHED

Beef is not the only story in the West, although you'd never know it from watching the typical oater or reading Louis L'Amour. Wool growers have played nearly as large a role in the written history of the West as cowboys, although admittedly they may not make for quite the same cigarette ad.

There are roughly 225,000 sheep in Montana (versus 2.6 million cows). Once a year in the spring, almost all those sheep need to be sheared. And while a sheep shearing isn't quite the same community effort as a good branding, it's still a chance to come together and share in a common labor.

Successfully shearing a sheep takes skill, training, and years of experience. Montana currently lays claim to only thirty or so sheep shearers who are good enough to be paid for their work. They're in high demand. In season, they travel from ranch to ranch, flipping sheep, switching out clipper blades, stitching up the occasional nick. The sheep, once they're in the midst of being shorn, are surprisingly docile. They just kind of hang out for a while, resigned.

Of the recommended things to do in this book, this is probably the least accessible for the average Joe. You can't pick up the phone and ask to go to a

A good shearer can shear a sheep in less than two minutes.

shearing. It needs a good connection to score the invitation. Nevertheless, if that invitation comes along, don't turn it down. You may be asked to herd some sheep into the chute, or perhaps use a push broom to clean the loose wool out of a shearing station. In return, you'll gain insight into where the wool in your winter coat comes from.

Kid Friendly

We're big believers in community labor. You only really feel like you're a part of a place if you put your shoulder to a common wheel. Kids will complain about having to work on a Saturday but they will finally be much happier for having invested the time.

13

TIP A SUNDAY AFTERNOON DRINK

Small-town saloons in Montana tend to be community centers as much as they are drinking establishments. They're the places where you gather to grab a burger and a beer, catch up on the gossip. The kids shoot pool while the grownups bitch about the weather and politics. (Most small town bars don't have a problem with kids hanging out until 9:00 p.m.) There are those who would rather spend a Sunday in church rather than brighten the world with a quick snort of tanglefoot, but we're not among them.

Blue noses notwithstanding, we don't know of any way to get to know Montana more readily than by spending a few hours in one of Montana's bars, striking up a conversation with a local rancher. Oil the social gears by buying a round. Pay for a shake-a-day then lay your quarters down on the rail. Talk about the local coyote derby or ask about the fishing. Leave your judgment at home.

When it comes to great saloons, Montana has so much to offer. There's The Murray,

Stacey's Old Faithful Bar & Grill in Gallatin Gateway has been around, under various owners, for nearly a century.

To play a game of pool, put your quarters on the rail during the game in progress. You'll have a chance to challenge the winner.

The Mint, and the Owl in Livingston. Up the Shields River, there's the Clyde Park Tavern, Wilsall's Bank Bar and Vault Restaurant, and, further up, the Ringling Bar. Stacey's in Gallatin Gateway has been around for more than ninety years and still offers a great Sunday afternoon vibe. Up in Pony, an old mining town in the Tobacco Roots, there's the Pony Bar. Columbus on the Yellowstone River supports the New Atlas Saloon. The Bear Creek Saloon between Red Lodge and Belfry has pig racing in season. If you're in the northwest, drop in on the Dirty Shame in the Yaak. There's the Sip 'n Dip Lounge in Great Falls. There's the Two Dot Bar in Two Dot, and

The Owl loung is one of Livingston's better known drinking establishments

the Montana Bar in Miles City. Don't forget Club Moderne in Anaconda. There's the Jimtown Bar out of Lame Deer, the Hell Creek Bar in Jordan, and, if you're feeling brave, Pisser's Palace in Walkerville.

Does it need to be said? No drinking and driving. Either draw straws to see who nurses Diet Coke for the evening or maybe get a motel room within walking distance.

Kid Friendly ★★☆☆☆

Some bars will be more receptive to kids shooting a game of pool than others. Stick your head in the door to get a sense for the vibe of the place before you commit.

MONTANA'S BREW PUBS

As of this writing, there are 113 brewpubs in Montana. That puts us second in the nation in terms of per capita breweries. This is due, at least in part, to the state's liquor licensing laws. In order to traditionally sell beer and wine, you need to draw a license by lottery or pay way too much on the secondary market. Liquor licenses, same deal. But if you brew beer, you can sell it in an attached tap room without those larcenous permits. There are restrictions in place (you can't serve after 8:00 p.m., for one), but the brewery loophole has encouraged some exceptional beers to be brewed in Montana.

FURTHER SUGGESTIONS FOR SPRING

Make a Pilgrimage to a Buffalo Jump

Buffalo jumps, of course, are those places wherein Montana's first residents hunted bison by herding them over a cliff. Take a hike and read an interpretive sign, enjoy the view and the breeze.

Take a Wildflower Hike

Choose a hike based on how open the trail is, or the altitude based on how cool the nights have been. Buy a guide book and take your camera.

Bike Going to the Sun Road Before It's Open to Cars

It's an annual feat of engineering, clearing the snow off the top of Glacier. Before the famous Going to the Sun Highway is open to motorized travel, it's available to intrepid peddlers.

Photograph Snow Geese on Freezeout Lake

In late March or early April, Freezeout Lake outside of Augusta, Montana, funnels in unbelievable swarms of migrating waterfowl, especially snow geese. It's a great photo opportunity, although hard to catch the timing just right.

SUMMER

The problem with summer in Montana is that it goes by too fast. Every weekend is precious and fleeting, accelerated by its own possibilities. You're only limited by your imagination, the gas in your tank, the tread on your tires, and the health of your credit card. Through a certain lens, it's kind of a burden. In the face of so many possible choices, how do you even begin to *carpe* that *diem*?

If you've been around a while, and in the face of the newest influx of folks, the biggest adjustment is planning. You can't run your summers on a whim anymore. The primo camping spots have to be reserved six months in advance, for instance. But if you have just a modicum of foresight, there's no reason you can't still seize the Montana day like a boss.

Pick a weekend, any weekend, then throw a dart. We're going to do *this*. The good news? There's no wrong choice.

14

FLY FISH THE YELLOWSTONE RIVER WITH A GUIDE

The Yellowstone River is the longest undammed river in the lower-forty-eight. It flows north out of Yellowstone Lake, over the Upper and Lower Falls, then continues north past Gardiner, through Yankee Jim Canyon in Paradise Valley (a tight fit, like a thumb pressed over a hose), and then toward Livingston, where it takes a sharp turn toward its rendezvous with the Missouri. From the park until a stretch well below Big Timber, the Yellowstone is clear enough, cold enough, capricious enough, to support a generous population of wild trout. It's got tight turns, drops in elevation that will put a twist in your stomach, some fairly technical white water, and fishing that's still pretty damn close to what you would have found a generation or two ago—keeping in mind that most of the marquee trout species we're familiar with today were introduced. Rainbows, browns, and brookies are all strangers in these waters. Only cutthroat trout and bull trout (technically a char) are Montana natives, as is the much-maligned whitefish.

Flies can be expensive, but remember that you're also buying access to the fly shop's expertise. Don't be afraid to ask for advice.

The Yellowstone River, south of Livingston, flows through one of the most gorgeous valleys in America.

There aren't as many fish per square mile in the Yellowstone as there are in, say, the Bighorn or the Missouri below Holter. But the possibility for enormous fish, for true lunkers, is as real on the Yellowstone as anywhere you'll fish. You never know what you're going to drag to the surface. Every year, the local newspaper runs a photo of some retiree lifting up, with some effort, an eleven-pound brown, all his otherwise questionable life choices suddenly vindicated.

The Yellowstone can be a tricky river to fish, though. And every year, runoff moves the gravel bars back and forth, cuts new channels, migrates the holding water east to west, north to south. Even if you've fished it before, it's not the same river you knew last year. That's part of the appeal, and part of the challenge. Hence: Hire a guide.

If you're an experienced fisherman, particularly a fly fisherman, with some measure of ego and identity wrapped up in the notion of your own accomplishments, it's natural to resist the notion that you have something to learn, that there's somebody out there so much better at this that they could teach you a few things. But guides know their rivers, they know the water, the flies, the hatch cycles. Even the best fisherman in the world, when confronted with new water, could benefit from a good guide. You spent all this money getting here, took time off work, so you really should spend a few hundred bucks to put a sheen on it. Consider at least half a day. Pick up the pointers, get a sense for how the fish use the water, then bounce off into the next day by yourself.

There are a number of good fly shops in the Livingston and Bozeman area, most of whom outfit on the Yellowstone. We recommend reserving a spot at least a few months in advance. If you wait until the last minute, you may still get a guide, but it probably won't be the most experienced guide in the outfitter's Rolodex. Those guys get booked up first.

If you feel like gambling a bit, you can also try to plan your trip around the famous Mother's Day caddis fly hatch. Every year, sometime in May, when the water temperature hits a certain

HELPFUL TIP

In addition to the Mother's Day caddis hatch, Southwest Montana hosts some epic salmonfly hatches. These enormous bugs show up around late May or early June, which means, more often than not, the hatch coincides with a time when the rivers are too brown to fish. But if you can catch the hatch just right, it will be the best dry-fly fishing of your life

threshold and the days are of a certain length, the caddis erupt on the Yellowstone. And that's exactly the right word: erupt. The number of bugs on the water? They look like floating pieces of carpet. And the same stretch of water that you beat your rod against last month, the feed lines that seemed absolutely barren of life, now they're one long ellipse of rising fish. Dot after dot after dot.

The trick for a nonresident fisherman, however, is in planning your trip. It's no cinch to try to catch the peak of the hatch. A few days on either side, too early or too late, and you might miss it entirely. Ask for advice from the fly shop, and then cross your fingers.

Kid Friendly

Bring a spinning rod, even though your guide might protest (there's an occasional, not very attractive bias among fly-fishermen against traditional tackle), and encourage rock skipping and swimming.

THE UNDAMMED YELLOWSTONE

THE LONGEST FREESTONE river in America owes its continuing freedom to a grassroots effort to oppose what was once called the Allenspur Dam. Dating back to 1962, the project would have put a hydroelectric dam on the Yellowstone south of Livingston, roughly where Carter's Bridge is now.

The efforts to oppose the dam were spearheaded by the late Montana author and conservationist James Posewitz, and included efforts by local fly-fishermen, including Dan Bailey. Posewitz in particular helped place a ten-page photo essay in a 1978 *Life* magazine, celebrating the Yellowstone River. That essay helped tip the scales of public opinion.

15

PAN FOR GOLD OR SAPPHIRES

On the surface, it would seem like one of the most touristy things you could possibly do. Gold panning. Pay someone for the opportunity to fill a saucer full of wet sand, swirl it around, see what's settled to the bottom. But here's the thing: It's not a cinch, panning for gold. You need a coach. You've got to get the wrist right, get the motion of the pan just so. Swirling sandy sludge back and forth, giving the heavier gold a chance to settle, having the patience to sift through the pebbles that

Panning for gold isn't a cinch. It needs an experienced guide to show you how to swirl the pan.

remain, having the eye to judge whether what's in your pan is the genuine article or the lighter, no-less-glittery fool's gold. But once you get the hang of it, it's quite satisfying: "Is that...maybe that's...I think that might be..."

Once you've got the trick of it, once you've found a few flakes of this soft, malleable metal, once you can understand the attraction—money just laying around in the ground, waiting to be found—then maybe you can go off on your own.

It's been one of the drivers of western expansion, after all. If it weren't for the long-shot hope of striking it rich, much of Montana initially wouldn't have been settled.

Factoid

Mining is still one of the economic drivers of Montana. The eight largest mines in the state are responsible, directly and indirectly, for creating more than 12,300 jobs. In a year, they help the state realize more than $200 million in revenue.

In addition to gold panning, there's the similar hunt for sapphires. The action is different—picking through a pile of gravel with tweezers—but the sensibility is the same.

Kid Friendly

They may resist initially, but even the most jaded, video-game addled child will dig into the idea of searching through a pile of drab rock for glittering gold or sapphires

16

LISTEN TO THE GHOSTS IN BANNACK

Montana has its share of famous and well-preserved ghost towns. It's the virtue of a relatively thin written history. You don't have to dig too far before you hit bedrock.

Honestly, though, we've always been a little lukewarm about the whole ghost-town experience. Abandoned buildings, rusting farm equipment, a cook stove missing its lids. They're an opportunity for reflection ("Look on my works, ye mighty, and despair!"), but the experience wears thin in short order. Consider: You seldom feel the urge to go *back* to a ghost town.

Still, you need to go once. This is, after all, where Montana began. There's Garnet and Landusky, Marysville and Zortman, Nevada City, Castle Town, Elkhorn, and Fort Assiniboine. That list goes on, with each town in its own unique stage of rehabilitation or dissolution. There may be locals still hanging on by their fingernails or out-of-staters determined to put in a B&B. There might be a bar with the Budweiser sign

Hand-hewn logs still show the marks of the adz that was used to flatten their sides.

At its acme, Bannack was home to at least three thousand gold-feverish residents.

still lit, a church advertising a spaghetti dinner, or weeds growing up through what used to be a school room floor. Regardless, you'll certainly hear the wind, some ground squirrels chirping. A creaking door. Pay attention to your own melancholy tug. There were lives being lived here. All the usual portfolios of hopes and dreams and disappointments, scornful dismissals and pleas for forgiveness. Also, man, how much work must have gone into that fireplace?

An exception to our dismissive and objectionable "nobody revisits a ghost town" idea is the Montana State Park of Bannack. There are older communities in Montana (Fort Benton goes back to 1847), but few that played as colorful a role in shaping the state's early history. Founded in 1862 when gold was found in nearby Grasshopper Creek, within a year, there were as many as three thousand tough, trigger-happy, gold-besotted souls living here. Two years later, Bannack was briefly named the first territorial capital of Montana. Within the span of those few years, there were road agents and vigilantes, murders, public trials, lynchings, sheriffs gone bad, and millions of dollars in gold gone missing.

To fully appreciate Bannack, fold it into a trip to Nevada City and Virginia City. The histories are intertwined. And be sure to read *A Decent, Orderly Lynching* by Frederick Allen. There's camping close by, including a handful of first-come first-served sites.

Ghost towns. Scratch them off your list, but wrap them into another activity. Bring along a bird book or a wildflower book, a pair of binoculars. Certainly a camera. Grab a picnic lunch and eat it in the middle of the street, just because you can.

Kid Friendly

There are very few kid-friendly amenities in Bannack (no ice cream trucks, for instance), but your children should enjoy being given free rein to run through the sixty different buildings, including an abandoned hotel and a schoolhouse.

The Masonic Lodge in Bannack is maintained by current-day Masons.

THE PIONEERS

Just down the road from Bannack is the southern start of the Pioneer Mountains Scenic Byway, forty-nine miles of state highway bisecting one of the cooler little ranges in the state. Among it's virtues? Elkhorn Hot Springs, just up the road from the little town of Polaris, and the Mom-and-Pop ski hill, Maverick Mountain. Further along, there's Crystal Park National Recreation Area. This 220-acre hillside kind of looks like a bomb went off, but in a good way. Imagine a minefield if every mine had already been accidentally triggered. The holes and mounds come from years of the general public digging with hand tools, trying to uncover some of the six-sided quartz crystals that famously formed in the area. The crystals have little value beyond conversation pieces on your coffee table, but the kids go bonkers for them.

This road closes in the winter, but stays open for snowmobilers and cross-country skiers. It's supposed to be excellent on both counts.

The quartz crystals to be dug up in Crystal Park include purple amethyst, above. If you follow the scenic byway north and then take a left, you'll eventually find Wisdom.

Great Montana Weekends

TAKE AN ARTFUL PHOTO IN YELLOWSTONE OR GLACIER

When it's not being flooded, Yellowstone National Park sees more than four million visitors a year, most of them in the summer, and most with some sort of camera. Statistically, however, very few of them stray more than a few feet off the boardwalks. Not only are they recording what is effectively the same experience over and over again, they're missing the best part of Yellowstone—hiking through one of the most pristine wildernesses in the lower forty-eight.

For new visitors to Yellowstone, the crowds might come as a surprise. Speeding a little too fast around a corner, you'll have to brake hard for the traffic jam of RVs lined up beside a buffalo bull chewing its cud. It's you and a couple hundred other folks throwing elbows to get a clear shot. Somehow, not surprisingly, the image on your phone isn't exactly *Geographic* quality. In order to have a chance at scoring a good photo, you really need to take a hike. And ideally you should do it in the very early morning or late in the evening, with a full-frame camera and a 400 mm lens, at least.

After you've seen Old Faithful, plan at least one early morning excursion into the backcountry. Hopefully you've brought a good DSLR with you. Twist a decent telephoto lens onto it, strap a tripod to your backpack, get your bear spray ready, and start walking. A lot of animals will go

The Lamar Valley offers numerous photo opportunities, and Grand Prismatic Spring, right, makes for good people-watching.

Goose Island in Glacier is one of the most photographed locations in Montana. Glacier's Lake Sherburne, left, is easily accessed by Route 3.

PHOTO BEST PRACTICES

To take the best possible photo, you need to check off a few basic boxes. Start with a full-frame DSLR or mirrorless camera. "Full-frame" means the sensor is the size of a traditional 35 mm negative, as opposed to the thumbtack-sized sensors in your phone. You can buy an early model quite affordably. We shoot with a Canon 6D, which is currently available used Online for $250.

Next, score a decent lens. Quality glass is going to cost you, but you should be able to find something for less than $1,000. For wildlife, we shoot a Sigma 150-600 mm that costs around $900. When paired with a tripod, it does the job just fine. Landscapes tend to be shot with wider angles. Look for a 16 mm or 35 mm.

Learn the basics of composition, aperture, shutter speed, and ISO. Google the rule of thirds. Then try to be shooting before everyone else is out of bed.

Finally, take an Online course in Photoshop or Lightroom. These days, the last coat of polish on most images comes after the fact, on the computer.

---

to timber during the day and come out to feed in the evenings, so your best chance for a good wildlife shot will likely come not only when the light is at its richest (the hour after sunrise, the hour before sunset) but when the animals are on their feet, moving through these transition periods.

Try a hike into Slough Creek in the Lamar Valley. There are three large meadows as you move progressively further up the trail. If you're in decent shape, a day hike should get you easily up and back to the first meadow. (But seriously, watch out for grizzlies. The bears love Slough Creek.) After Slough, consider hanging out with the wolf watchers above the highway in the Lamar. You might get lucky. When all else fails, the Grizzly Discovery Center in West Yellowstone has captive wolves and bears.

Glacier National Park, in our opinion, is a case study, in real time, for what's been called the tragedy of the commons. Too often that phrase has been used to advocate for private control of public resources, but in the case of Glacier, it's an apt description for what happens when too many people rush to enjoy an ephemeral, fragile resource. It's one of the conundrums of the New West. When solitude and wilderness are the commodities, being here to take part means taking part in its loss.

> **HELPFUL TIP**
>
> *Keep your distance from wildlife. Yellowstone regulations require that you stay at least one hundred yards from grizzlies and wolves, and twenty-five yards from most large animals, including elk and bison. Even that feels kind of close, honestly.*

Glacier is accessed by three main roads. North Fork Road out of Polebridge on the west side, Route 3 to Many Glacier on the east side, and the famous thruway, Going-to-the-Sun Road. In peak season, reservations to the park are now required.

If you care to compete for the resource, there are some fantastic landscapes to be found in Glacier. Get up early and take a hike, maybe try to camp in the backcountry. Lake McDonald, on the west side, has multi-colored rocks in the lake bed. Catch it on a quiet evening with a polarized lens and a tripod—you'll get one of the landscape shots of your life. Goose Island on the east side is one of the more photographed locations in America. There's a parking lot for the viewing platform, and you'll probably be part of a crowd, jockeying for position.

Wildlife in Glacier is a little harder to come by. If you can score a parking spot on Logan Pass, try to hike down into Hidden Lake. There might be some habituated bighorn sheep who will strike a pose. And there's always a good chance for some mountain goats.

If all else fails, consider photographing other tourists. Photography as an art form is particularly suited to portraiture. As viewers, we're drawn to someone else's face, and hardwired to respond to the emotion they're experiencing. Turn your camera around and get a candid shot of someone else being moved by the landscape.

Kid Friendly

Most kids don't seem to understand the impulse to shoot photos. They are tolerant and patient, until they're not.

GALLATIN PETRIFIED FOREST

NORTH OF YELLOWSTONE, the Gallatin Petrified Forest represents more than 50 million years of history. Volcanoes erupting during the Eocene helped preserve standing forests. This didn't happen in one event but rather several times. The fossil fields in this site are more than two thousand feet thick.

To reach the forest, you'll need to take a hike. Google Tom Miner Campground in the Gallatin National Forest. The trailhead starts just off the campground. A short hike offers an interpretive trail with some posted signs. A longer hike will take you deeper into the petrified forest.

18

VISIT ART IN THE WIND

You ever wake up with a hankering for an outdoor art installation? Sure, sure you have. And Montana's got you.

In Missoula, a self-guided walking tour lists twenty-eight separate art pieces. If you're in Bozeman, check out Gallatin Art Crossing Online, including their interactive map. The pieces at the public library on the east side of town are especially noteworthy. Downtown Billings has a similar public art map. In Whitefish, a solid day could be filled just bouncing between the moose sculptures. But the two most conspicuous jewels in this particular crown are outside of Lincoln and not far from Fishtail.

First, there's Lincoln. Take a look at Blackfoot Pathways: Sculpture in the Wild. It's a world-class walking

Ponderosa Whirlpool
by Chris Drury

Re-Imagining the Delaney Sawmill TeePee Burner *by Kevin O'Dwyer*.

park that just about nails Western Montana's cultural and natural history. At once a tribute to the region's industrial base as well as a commentary on contemporary culture, here's an exhibit that really could exist nowhere else. Visiting artists are invited to come to Lincoln, spend time in the area, then create exhibits that reflect and interpret the experience. There are artists and composers in residence, and there's an emphasis on community outreach and service. The local schools are notable beneficiaries.

The whole thing is set in timber that looks to have been strategically thinned. You start out inside a repurposed "teepee burner." These conical structures were used, back in the day, to burn sawdust and wood waste. Anywhere there were active lumber yards in Montana, you'd see teepee burners. From there, you move on to exhibits like *Picture Frame* by Jaakko Pernu (a large tilted box that invites you to consider tree branches as art form) and *Tree Circus* by Patrick Dougherty, a woven structure large enough to walk through. Personal favorites include *House of Sky* by Alan Counihan (a mirror box set on stilts), and *Ponderosa Whirlpool* by Chris Drury.

Blackfoot Pathways was founded by members of the community, and was built largely on donations. It's rooted in generosity, and it shows. Generous of spirit, accessible, free to the public with very few restrictions (you can even take your leashed dog for a walk around the sculptures), it's an unqualified good for Lincoln and for Montana.

Two Disks *by Alexander Calder, above, and* Xylem *by Francis Kéré, right, are both displayed at Tippet Rise.*

A long drive south and east, the Tippet Rise Art Center out of Fishtail, just north of the Absaroka-Beartooth Wilderness, sits on twelve thousand acres of private ranch, and makes for an interesting complement and contrast to Blackfoot Pathways. Gravel roads wind around outdoor performance spaces and large sculptures from internationally famous artists. There are bus tours, and hiking or mountain biking from sculpture to sculpture is encouraged. Access can be quite limited, however, particularly during peak season and without reservations.

In season, some of the world's finest classical musicians present a rotating series of concerts, indoors and out. Alas, you're unlikely to be able to see one of these performances. You put your name in for a lottery and, if you're drawn, you will be awarded the privilege of buying a ticket.

Some of the same well-intentioned folks involved with Tippet Rise have, according to Online sources, also been instrumental in helping manage Storm King, an outdoor sculpture garden a couple of hours outside of New York City. And while Storm King is one of our favorite places on the East Coast, we honestly have mixed feelings about Tippet Rise. What works so well in the tight hills and deciduous forests of the Hudson Valley, in our opinion, may not translate quite as well to the West. Tippet Rise is sited on some of the most gorgeous, awe-inspiring, jaw-droppingly lovely landscape in the world. Mountains that come up off the foothills to punch you in the nose with waterfalls and crumbling peaks and unbroken sweeps of old-growth pine forest. It is sublime and humbling and deeply spiritual. And in our opinion, we're just not sure that a Calder plopped down in front of it necessarily improves the view. The property also sits on land that was

> **Factoid**
>
> *There aren't that many large art museums in Montana (Missoula, Billings, and Great Falls), but there are tons of art galleries. Every small town has at least a few. Even if you're not in the market, galleries offer a great opportunity for browsing. And if you hit them during a Friday night art walk, you might get a free glass of wine or some toothpick* hors d'oeuvres.

once owned and ranched by Isabelle Johnson, an important modernist painter and a pivotal figure in the history and development of Montana's arts scene. And while Tippet Rise tips its hat toward Johnson with a website page and a couple of paintings hanging in their performance space, the Olivier Music Barn, she is not given the consideration that, in our opinion, she fully deserves. This used to be *her* ranch. They should have named the whole damn place after her.

Tippet Rise is worth a visit, certainly, if you can swing it. But go to Lincoln first.

Kid Friendly

It's the unusual child who appreciates any sort of art at first glance, but with some context and coaching and cajoling, and in the case of Blackfoot Pathways, the freedom to climb around on an exhibit or two, there's plenty of opportunity to expand some horizons.

WHAT'S IN A NAME?

NOTHING SETS A VISITOR APART quite like the mispronunciation of a name. Here in Montana, the Capitol city is pronounced Hell-uh-nuh, not Hell-ee-nuh. Growing up in Livingston, we'd go hunting in the Ub-zore-keys, not Ab-suh-roke-uhs (this one's a little bit of a tossup, whether it's keys or kuhs, but I'll go to bat for my usage). It's Glass-go, not Glass-gow, Sidney is spelled with an I not a Y, Harlo is short for Harlowton, Nez Pierce not Nay Per-se, and Meagher County is pronounced Mar, not Meager. Depuyer is De-poo-yer, Kootenai is Koot-nee, and Pondera County is Pahn-duh-ray.

Pompous ass is pronounced pretty much like it's spelled.

19

CLIMB A PEAK

If you live in or visit Western Montana, most of your time is going to be spent within sight of the mountains. If you're fortunate, you can see them from your living room window. Driving to work, idling at a stoplight, there they are. That scalloped horizon. At your keyboard, glancing up...Wonder what the snow pack's looking like this year? In the evenings, after the valleys have fallen into shadow, the peaks will still glow for a moment. They're your last glimpse of the day just passed and your first glimpse of the morning to come.

Fairy Lake in the Bridgers lies just below Sacagawea Peak.

From the Sacagawea Peak Trail saddle in the Bridgers, looking down over Gallatin Valley, you can see Sacagawea Peak (left) as well as Pomp Peak (right).

These mountains are such an essential part of our lives, it's more or less incumbent on you to get out into them as often as possible. And we all spend so much time looking at the highest points, it feels like an additional obligation to climb at least one of them, at least once. That peak there. Remember what it was like to stand on top of it? Did it make you feel...substantial? Significant?

Not far from Bozeman, one of our favorite hikes is up to Sacagawea Peak in the Bridgers. You begin at 7,700 feet at Fairy Lake (after a six-mile kidney bruiser of a drive on washboard gravel), and then it's around a 2.6-mile hike to the peak, the highest point in the Bridgers. The crowds can be substantial (parking at Fairy Lake fills up), but the views of Gallatin Valley are worth it. Try to go during the week if you can. And Google road openings before you make the drive. The road to Fairy Lake always seems to take a while to open.

Kid Friendly

There are peaks and then there are peaks. If hiking with kids, be cautious about the routes you choose, and have realistic expectations. It's always okay to turn around.

DESTINATION HIKING

THERE ARE, OF COURSE, any number of informed regional guide books to help you build a decent weekend. In our family, it's not unusual for us to set off with three or four of them rattling around in the backseat. One of the things we've found, especially hiking with kids, is that it's beneficial to have some sort of destination in mind. The eight- or ten-year-old brain can't quite wrap itself around the idea of hiking for the sake of hiking. They need to have a purpose. And when it comes to manufactured purpose, nothing beats a waterfall. One of our favorite books in this regard, naturally enough, is *Hiking Waterfalls in Montana,* by John Kratz. If you're in Bozeman, consider Grotto Falls up Hyalite. If you're in Missoula, there's Cascade Falls outside of Plains, or maybe Abha Falls off Bass Creek Trail in the Bitterroot Mountains.

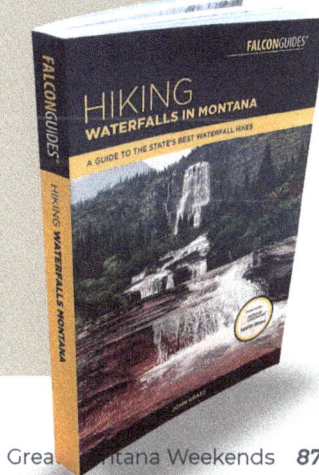

20

HIKE UNDERGROUND

If you attend elementary school in Montana, east of the divide but west of Billings, you will eventually be taken on a field trip to Lewis and Clark Caverns. Our twelve-year-old son has been at least three times now.

South of the interstate between Whitehall and Three Forks, this small but colorful cave system makes for a perfect, kid-friendly day trip. Combine it with a picnic next to the Jefferson River or a day hike around the state park. Above ground, there are ten miles' worth of hiking trails. Maybe spend the night in the campground. Watch for rattlesnakes.

After a switch-backy drive from Highway 2, you'll park at a state facility. The larger park is open year-around, but the caves are only open from May 1 to September 30. Tickets for cave tours can be reserved Online. An easy, mile-plus hike from the interpretive center takes you to the cavern entrance. There are at least three tours. The two-hour "Classic Cave Tours" might be the place to start.

Kid Friendly ★★★★★

As cave tours go, Lewis and Clark Caverns are accessible and edifying. The tour guides know their history and enjoy their work. Grandparents who have trouble with stairs, or kids in strollers, should be cautious.

Karen Kenyon

21

PICK SOME FLATHEAD CHERRIES

Montana has a handful of notable microclimates, little pockets wherein altitude and topography conspire to produce unique pieces of weather. Parts of the Bitterroot, for instance, are particularly suited to growing apples. And the town of Three Forks, west of Bozeman, is especially arid, receiving hardly any snow compared to Bozeman. Then there's Flathead Lake. A combination of moisture and relatively mild winter temperatures provides the perfect place, it turns out, for growing cherries. And they're so good. If you're on your deathbed in June, try to stick around at least until the end of July. You'll want to try this year's crop.

Driving around Flathead Lake in late July and early August, especially on the east side, you'll see a number of roadside cherry stands, one after the other. Most every orchard seems to prop up a hand-painted sign and hires a teenager to stand watch over their flats. Used to be, buying cherries in bulk from the orchards meant saving a

> **HELPFUL TIP**
>
> *Polson, Montana, on the south end of Flathead Lake, has a cherry festival every summer at the end of July or first part of August. It's delicious, unironic Americana, complete with pie eating contests, pit-spitting contests, and vendor booths.*

The orchards around Flathead Lake take advantage of the local microclimate to grow some of the sweetest cherries you'll find.

ton of money. Anymore, however, it seems like the prices don't really reflect the venue. Alas, the cherries from the roadside vendors are often as pricey as the cherries you might get from a grocery store.

To really see some savings, you'll need to pick your own. And if you have kids, there's really no better way to spend a Saturday or Sunday afternoon. Bring your camera. (We have photos of our nieces from twenty years ago. The girls with cherry juice smeared all over their faces, dimpled chins to eyebrows. So damn adorable.)

You have to plan ahead, though. There aren't a lot of places that still allow you to pick your own cherries. We've been told it might have something to do with liability insurance. And indeed, climbing around on ladders with a bucket is risky. Nevertheless, if you're nimble enough…

Kid Friendly

Climbing on ladders is dangerous. Eating fruit with pits is dangerous. Hanging out with wasps and bees is dangerous. Caveats in place, and after insisting that the ladders are for grownups, let the kids babysit the bucket as you pick. Cherries are high fiber, so also make sure you're close to a bathroom later.

22

GO CAR CAMPING

If you've ever been backpacking—serious backpacking, three or four days, maybe a week in the mountains—you understand the importance of weight. Measuring out the pounds, the ounces, that go into your pack. The first mile, there's not a whole lot of difference between forty-five and fifty pounds. But ten miles back, you start resenting every ounce. And by the time you get home, you've pared it down to bare-bones essentials. I mean, why *did* you bring along those nail clips?

In that context, the notion of car camping is almost criminal in its luxuriousness. Back your truck up to the open garage and just toss in that six-man tent. Air mattress. Maybe a bottle of lighter fluid. The Coleman stove and camp chairs. Pans and pots. Finally, the cooler full of eggs, steak, bacon, lunch meat, beer. It's hard to appreciate how much fun car camping can be until you've gone backpacking a few times.

In any case, when it comes to improved campgrounds, Montana has it made. The fringes of every chunk of national forest are dotted, on maps, with helpful little camping icons. There are

Some people buy maps to help them travel. Other folks travel in order to buy maps.

Some of the best campsites in Montana need strategic planning. This site on the east side of Glacier was reserved six months ahead.

state campgrounds, national forest campgrounds, and private outfits (KOAs). The national forest campgrounds can be reserved six months in advance at recreation.gov. Our recommendation would be to make your choice based first on how much time you have and how far you're willing to drive. Much better to get off the beaten path if you can. Nothing sucks so hard as driving thirty minutes up a washboardy gravel road, maybe pulling a trailer (with all the accompanying anxiety about maneuverability and flat tires), only to find, when you get there, that the campground is full. Maybe leave on Thursday rather than Friday afternoon. And take a look at the Pintlars rather than the Gallatins. Ideally, find a place that has a stream big enough to fish, maybe a lake with brookies for the frying pan.

If you have kids, throw in some mountain bikes as well. A Frisbee. A cornhole toss. But please do not—for the love of god, do *not*—bring a stereo to play in the campground. If you're that devoted to your music, throw in some headphones. But have a little courtesy. There's nothing so rude as imposing your music on the nice folks camping right next door. Most of us go to the woods to get away from other people's music.

Kid Friendly

Plan ahead with bikes, games, Frisbees, etc., and either leave the devices at home or strategically let the batteries drain.

CAR CAMPING CHECKLIST

DEPENDING ON YOUR SITUATION, every family will have a slightly different set of car-camping needs. The list below works for us:

- Tent
- Sleeping bags
- Pillows
- Inflatable mattress
- Headlamps
- Firewood, fire starter
- Matches
- Change of clothes
- Toiletries
- Pocket knife, ax
- Sunscreen
- Bug dope
- Collapsible chairs
- Towels, washcloths, soap
- Tarps
- Water jugs
- First-aid kit
- Batteries
- Rope
- Lantern for table
- Tablecloth and clamps
- Camera, tripod
- Coleman stove, fuel
- Frying pan, pot
- Plates, plastic ware, mugs
- Paper towels
- Toilet paper
- Salt, pepper
- Cooler with eggs, bacon, sandwich stuff
- S'mores
- Ground coffee, French press
- Sponge, dishtowel, soap
- Extra blanket
- Books
- Maps
- Hat, gloves, bathing suit
- Bear spray

23

WATCH A BIRD

The older we get, the more we've come to appreciate that superficially absurd notion of bird watching. In our twenties, it just felt like a silly way to spend your time. Passively sitting back with the binoculars to do…what, exactly? Try to put a name to one of those little brown jobs fluttering around in the chokecherries? Our thirties, being able to identify a given bird became part of a larger obligation toward knowing our place in the world. That's a ponderosa pine not a Douglas fir, those are bobcat tracks not coyote tracks, and…could that really be an immature goshawk? Cool. Our forties, identification became a bit more serious, and when someone's life list topped out over five hundred species, it was an accomplishment to be admired. Now in our fifties, it's entirely possible that we will start structuring trips around the spotting of rare transients. Birdwatching is the bomb, man.

Best places to spot an interesting bird in Montana? As a start, there's the Owen Sowerwine Natural Area east of Kalispell (riparian bottomland managed by the Flathead Audubon and Montana Audubon societies), while thirty miles west of Kalispell

There may be as many as 433 different species of birds that spend time in Montana, including the American goldfinch, right.

The Red Rock Lakes National Wildlife Refuge is a remote but rewarding destination for birders.

is the 8,800-acre Lost Trail National Wildlife Refuge.

In the Mission Valley, there's the Ninepipe National Wildlife Refuge, great for waterfowl and shorebird viewing (there have been as many as two hundred different species spotted here), while south of Missoula, along the Bitterroot, there's Lee Metcalf Wildlife Refuge, 2,800 acres of meditational quiet after the cacophony of Reserve Street.

In early to mid-March, Freezout Lake Wildlife Management Area south of Choteau serves as a staging area for snow geese migrations. As many as three hundred thousand snow geese and ten thousand tundra swans will hang out for a while before continuing on.

One of the better birdwatching locations in the state, if you have the time, is Red Rock Lakes National Wildlife Refuge west of West Yellowstone and east of Lima. It's a

Yellow-headed blackbirds, sandhill cranes, and meadowlarks can all be spotted in Montana.

high elevation wetlands (6,600 feet), and is home to any number of interesting birds, including long-billed curlews in the meadows and white-faced ibises in the marshes. You're quite a ways from civilization here, though, so be sure you have a full tank of gas and a full cooler.

Kid Friendly ★★★☆☆

It would be the rare kid who might see the virtues in bird watching. But make sure they have their own set of binoculars and then turn them loose. You never know....

FERAL HOUSE CATS

IF YOU WERE TO make a list of the gravest threats to wild birds in Montana, feral house cats would be at the top. According to the American Bird Conservancy, predation by domestic cats "is the number one direct, human-caused threat to birds in the United States and Canada. ... In the United States alone, outdoor cats kill approximately 2.4 billion birds every year." House cats are adorable, and valued members of our families. But if you have a cat, do a bird a favor and keep it indoors.

24

FOLLOW A DINOSAUR TRAIL

We're not telling anyone the news when we say that Montana is full of fossils.

The world's first *Tyrannosaurus rex* was found in 1902 near Jordan. Egg Mountain near Choteau is the site of the first discovered dinosaur embryos, as well as one of the largest concentrations of dinosaur skeletons in the world. (A large herd of *Maiasaura* apparently all died together in a cataclysmic event some 76 million years ago.) The former Curator of Paleontology at the Museum of the Rockies, Jack Horner, was heavily involved in the *Maiasaura* find, and was also, not incidentally, scientific advisor for the first few "Jurassic Park" movies.

The Montana Dinosaur Trail is a cool, if admittedly chamber-of-commercy, acknowledgment of this exceptional dinosaur heritage, as well as an attempt to place some kind of tourist-friendly structure on it. If you Google it, you'll see a map with fourteen museums and facilities listed, scattered all across Montana. Taken together, these sites make up the dino "trail." Locations include the Blaine County Museum in

As opposed to the pristine, solid artifacts you see in museums, dinosaur bones typically come out of the ground in fragile pieces.

Chinook, the Fort Peck Interpretive Center, and of course the Museum of the Rockies. If nothing else, it makes for a handy field guide for things to do in a given area of Montana.

Of more interest, perhaps, are the three facilities that offer public paleontology field dig opportunities. These include Two Medicine Dinosaur Center, Great Plains Dinosaur Museum, and the Carter County Museum. It's one thing to passively walk through a dinosaur museum, it's another to be actively involved in digging up some bones. Montana can do that for you.

If you're interested in a less institutional dig, you can also contact one of the small handful of folks who provide day trips to dig sites. A family friend in Garfield County, Clayton Phipps (cowboydinodigs.com), offers full-day and half-day trips.

Kid Friendly

Are you kidding? They're dinosaurs.

BONE PICKERS

Montana has its share of compelling subcultures—groups that have self-identified according to occupation or compulsion. Just offhand, there are the climbers, the skiers, the dope-smokers (with some generous overlap between the smokers and climbers), the cutting-horse folks, the landscape painters, the wildlife photographers, and so on. We are proud to belong to the dissolute and disreputable Montana writing community.

There's also the dinosaur-hunting community, made up of professional bone pickers who spend their days scouring the hills for crumbling, sixty-five-million-year-old pieces of eBay goodness. Fossils are scattered pretty much all across Montana, but the most famous area is probably the Hell Creek formation in the northeast. This is gumbo country—bentonite, shale, sandstone—and with each new rainstorm, another layer of clay is peeled back to reveal the next page of crumbling protrusions.

Bone hunters are not to be confused with the academics, the professors and graduate students who dig on behalf of research and publication. Indeed, there is little love lost between these two communities. The academics tend to dislike the private guys for putting their finds up for auction and so away from the public trust, while the private guys dislike the academics for perceived snootiness and the disregard they show for otherwise noteworthy finds.

It's unexpectedly complicated, bone hunting in Montana.

SING ALONG WITH THE ANTHEM AT A RODEO

Until the most recent generation, most small towns in Montana were isolated islands of self-reliance at the end of a railroad spur. Driving toward a small town, you'll still most often see the community's grain silo, lonesome beside a railroad track, before you see anything else. Given their isolation, the annual events for these communities, the celebrations, came to take on undue importance. It was a reason to get together in a communal setting, a reason to reaffirm connections and drink a few too many, blow off the steam of daily anxiety and reassure ourselves that, yeah, we're all really doing okay after all.

Karen Kenyon

A presentation of flags at the Livingston Roundup

Of the essential community celebrations (weddings, funerals, brandings), few have been as important as the summer rodeo. Spectator or participant, for Montanans the local rodeo has been an opportunity to show off (and reward) skills as a rancher and cowboy. These days, even though most ropers and rough-stock riders are professionals on the circuit, it's still possible, especially in the smaller towns, to see the amateurs go at it, to see friends and neighbors come out of the gate swinging a loop behind a calf.

If you're in Montana during the Fourth of July, you must—*must*—take in a rodeo, maybe a parade while you're

Bullfighters are the unsung heroes of rodeo. A kids' competition, mutton bustin', far left, can still be found at some of the smaller rodeos.

at it. Fireworks. Carney food. Maybe some mutton bustin' or nanny slammin'. Barrel racing and, of course, the bull riding. Livingston puts on a great show. So does Choteau. Also, Bigfork, Drummond, Ennis, Wilsall, Red Lodge, Arlee. Of these, the rodeo talent, the rough stock (bull riding, bareback, saddle bronc) may be the best in Livingston (although we admit to having some hometown bias here).

When picking your rodeo, look to see if it's a Professional Rodeo Cowboys Association (PRCA) sanctioned event. If so, this means that the riders get credit toward their year's winnings, important for the National Finals Rodeo in Vegas. PRCA rodeos will, for the most part, draw more talented riders. But the small-town rodeos are better for flavor, for personality, for a photo of a ranch kid in hat and boots and ketchup smeared across her cheeks.

For a great small-town ranch rodeo, consider the Brockway Dairy Day Rodeo (third weekend in July). Also, the Augusta American Legion Rodeo. Jordan throws a great one as well.

Kid Friendly

Clowns, horses, bulls, corn dogs? C'mon....

26

ROAD TRIP TO A MUSIC FESTIVAL

A pretty good summer could be had in Montana just bouncing from one music festival to the next.

The cool thing about a good music fest? How it filters the crowd. You stand back and look out over the hundreds, maybe thousands, of bobbing heads, and you know every one of them has the good sense to like quality music, and be willing to go to some trouble and expense to see it live. The *type* of music, of course, is a further filter. These are my people, is the idea. Here in Montana, you're going to see a different crowd at Rockin' the Rivers, say, than you'll see at Red Ants Pants.

Among the good handful of summer festivals across Montana, our favorite so far is Red Ants Pants out of White Sulphur Springs. Red Ants Pants is a homegrown business started by entrepreneur Sarah Calhoun in 2006 that manufactures work wear for women. From a small-business standpoint, her work is a model for what's still possible for one person to accomplish in America. Five years after opening her shop,

A good Montana music festival will have side events in addition to the music, often including things like crosscut competitions.

The Red Ants Pants festival outside of White Sulphur Springs draws some of the biggest names in country, folk, and bluegrass music.

Calhoun began Red Ants Pants Foundation, a nonprofit meant to support "women's leadership, working family farms and ranches, and rural communities." The music festival is an aspect of the Foundation. And over the years, some of the biggest names in country music have traveled to this dry, dusty cow pasture a few miles from White Sulphur. Merle Haggard, Lucinda Williams, Lyle Lovett, Dwight Yoakum, the list goes on. In 2019, pre-Covid, more than 16,000 people attended. Red Ants Pants usually takes place in late July.

A close second, or maybe tied for first, is the Montana

Headframes are those angular structures that sit above underground mines, powering the elevators that hoist materials up and down the shaft. In Butte, they're emblems of a bygone time.

Folk Festival in Butte. Held on the second full weekend in July, Friday to Sunday, the Folk Festival is a free event, designed by Butte's civic leaders as a way to help promote one of the funkiest and coolest towns in the West. This one doesn't draw quite the headliners as some other festivals, but what it lacks in curb appeal it makes up for in authenticity and style. Also, did we mention it's free?

Other Montana music festivals worth a quick Google include Under the Big Sky in Whitefish, Rockin' the Rivers in Three Forks, the Headwaters Country Jam also in Three Forks, Magic City Blues in Billings, and Big Sky Big Grass in Big Sky.

Kid Friendly

Even if kids aren't into the grownup music, many of the festivals will have family-oriented events associated with them. We highly recommend Red Ants Pants for families.

MONTANA MUSICIANS

THERE HAVE BEEN PLENTY of notable musicians who were either born in Montana or, at some point, called Montana home. Pianist Philip Aaberg lives up on the Hi-Line. Jeff Ament, bassist for Pearl Jam, was born in Havre and lives in Missoula. When Hoyt Axton passed away, he was living in Victor. Huey Lewis ("I Want a New Drug") hangs his hat outside of Stevensville. And Colin Meloy, of The Decemberists, was born and raised in Helena. (His sister, Maile Meloy, is a highly regarded novelist.) Charlie Pride lived in Great Falls, Helena, and Missoula while he was playing minor league baseball, and pianist George Winston grew up in Miles City.

27

RIDE A RENTED HORSE

Horses are a little bit like boats. Tempting to buy, expensive to keep, hard on a marriage, and impossible to finally let yourself sell. Better to get the horse thing out of your system with the occasional day ride. And in hunting season, when it comes time to pack out your elk…do the right thing and *borrow* a horse.

Summers, rented horses will likely be fairly gentle and well-behaved (since they're being ridden often), and the sore knees and blisters on your butt will only last a few days. There are any number of reputable day-ride outfits in Montana. It's probably hard to go too wrong for a few hours on a pleasant Saturday afternoon. Do appropriate due diligence, though, and then pick your ride based on location and online reviews. Figure out what part of Montana, Yellowstone, or Glacier you would like to see from the back of a horse, then gravitate in that direction. Helpful tip? Avoid booking more than a few hours. Your butt and knees will thank you.

Kid Friendly

The novelty of a horseback ride tends to wear off after an hour or two. And horses, no matter how tame, are always a little dangerous.

BUCKET LIST BACKCOUNTRY

No matter how much time you spend in Montana's backcountry, either on horseback or on foot, there's still more to see. It would be the work of a generous lifetime, hitting all the high spots.

First on the list of the places we've yet to visit is the Chinese Wall in the Bob Marshall Wilderness. Fifty-four footsore miles will get you from the trailhead outside of Augusta to the wall, then on to a car drop. One of the backcountry boxes we *have* managed to check is the twenty-six-mile "Beaten Path" point-to-point trail from the Cooke City side of the Beartooth Plateau to the East Rosebud. We did it over three days. We've heard it's possible to do it one if you're in really, really good shape. After the floods of 2022, however, the road to the East Rosebud is now a creekbed for the last few miles. Google current conditions before you plan a trip.

28

GO FOR A MOUNTAIN BIKE RIDE

If you live in the West long enough, you quickly come to distinguish between the different types of accessible public lands. Here in Montana, of course, trespassing on private land is verboten, particularly in hunting season. State lands, the smattering of square school sections around the state, are publicly owned but require a modest fee to the state for sportsman's access. (If you're a hunter or a fisherman, when you buy your conservation tag, an additional state lands access fee is one of the optional add-ons.) There are BLM sections and national wildlife refuges, both of them owned by the federal government and both operating under their own set of rules. Pursuing your recreational pleasure on this side of the fence rather than that—say you decide to shoot prairie dogs—could mean a hefty fine or even jail time, depending on which bureaucratic body administers the land.

If you're into mountain biking, the biggest distinction you need to keep in mind is between wilderness (roadless) areas, state lands, BLM, wildlife sanctuaries, and straight-up national forest. Much as you might like to spend a day on the fat tires in the Beartooths or the Pintlers, the Scapegoats or the Missions, you're out of

Ski resorts like Big Sky, above, often offer their lifts to mountain bikers.

luck. You might get a mile or so up the trail but then you'll see one of those wilderness area signs reminding you that wheeled travel is restricted. They want you to hoof it.

There's enough wilderness area, in fact, that it can feel like all the primo locations are taken. But take a look at the Bangtails outside of Bozeman, or the Elkhorns outside of Helena. Both small ranges with some excellent mountain biking to be had. There is also an excellent book, *Montana Singletrack: The Mountain Biker's Guide to Montana*, published by Beartooth Publishing (we're unaffiliated with the business, but fans of their work) that should serve as your starting point.

For an enjoyable, but pricey day, certain ski hills offer lift service for fat-tire enthusiasts. Some of them, like Discovery, include designed courses.

Kid Friendly

Bikes. Kids. Ski lifts. It's all good.

29

TUBE THE LOWER MADISON OR THE CLARK FORK

There's a lot to be said for the simpler pleasures in life. During the heat of a Montana summer day, there are few things so simple as putting an inflated inner tube in a cold river, plopping your butt backwards, and letting yourself get carried away by the current. Sun on your stomach, feet in the water, whenever you start to feel overheated, tilt off the tube and swim for a bit. After an hour or two, there's a kind of meditative stillness that comes over you. The river becomes a metaphor for, for, for…something. Something *big*. Life? Why not. Carrying you along with it, not quite helplessly. It'll be over before you know it. Enjoy it while it lasts, man.

Outside of Bozeman, the Lower Madison gets the heaviest tubing pressure, and Warm Springs to Black's Ford is by far the most popular stretch. Thirty-some years ago, they expanded the Warm Springs access, tripling the size of the parking lot, putting in the outhouses. At the time, we told friends it was a waste of money. "They're really overbuilding it. Way to spend those tax dollars, guys." But these days, driving past on Saturday afternoon in August, the parking lot is full and there might be cars spilling out onto the highway. One more indication that our ability to read the tea leaves is modest at best.

College kids love this stretch. You'll see flotillas of them, every group with its cooler full of beer, cheerfully drinking themselves into second-degree sunburns. If you have small children, we might recommend being a little cautious about this stretch during certain weekends. Maybe think about going earlier in the day, or maybe put in at Black's Ford and take out at Greycliff Campground. That float isn't quite as long, but shorter might also be a good thing with kids.

> **HELPFUL TIP**
>
> *If you are part of a small group, or only have one vehicle, you're going to need someone to shuttle your vehicle from put in to take out. Try calling one of the local fly shops for a shuttle recommendation. For a modest fee, an enterprising stranger will be happy to pick up your vehicle and then drop it off again a few miles down the road. It'll make you feel odd the first time you do it, but we've never had a problem.*

We're less familiar with the Missoula-area floats, but judging by some of the river traffic you can see from the Higgins Street bridge, there are plenty of folks with experience who can point you in the right direction.

Floating with kids, depending on their ages, you might want to rope your tubes together. Each kid gets her own space, but you never lose control of her tube. Find a hard-sided plastic cooler and rope it to one of the tubes,

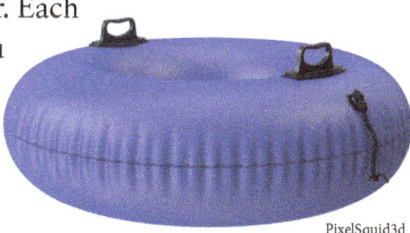

PixelSquid3d

Karen Kenyon

or perhaps rope the tubes into a circle with the cooler at the center. Mom and Dad have a cold beer close by, the kids have their juice and soda, the tube of sunscreen is floating around in the melted ice somewhere, and snacks are handy.

River traffic can be heavy at times. Be considerate. First and foremost, no glass bottles. If you're drinking beer or soda, make sure it's in cans. You don't want a barefoot floater cutting her feet on broken glass at the bottom of the river. Wear sneakers or sandals that won't come off (no flipflops) as you're going to spend some time walking on riverbottom gravel. And there's always that ass who forgets rule number one above. Also, suncreen. Lots of it, reapplied often. Probably a sunshirt, especially for the kids.

Paddling on the tube is a slow-moving affair. You lean back and flap your hands in the water. To really make a big change in trajectory, if the river is shallow you just stand up and carry your tube or pull it along behind you. If the water is too deep to touch bottom, you hold onto the tube with one hand and sidestroke along.

Kid Friendly

With caveats, and with appropriate parental caution regarding drunk college students, sunburns, and the swimming abilities of your kids, there are few better ways for a ten-year-old to spend a day in Montana than floating down a river on an inner tube.

30

VISIT THE CROW FAIR

One of our bucket-list items that we still haven't quite managed to pull of is the annual Crow Fair in Eastern Montana.

With a history that goes back to 1904, the Crow Fair has been called the "Tipi Capital of the World." From the third Thursday in August (open to the public on Friday) until Monday of the next week, as many as 1,500 tipis and 50,000 visitors come together outside of Crow Agency to celebrate the Apsáalooke people and culture. There's a rodeo, parade, and powwow. Tipi rentals are available.

If you go, remember that you're a guest. Do some due diligence with regard to proper behavior. Enjoy yourself, but pay appropriate respect.

Kid Friendly

From other powwows we've attended, kids and grownups from all backgrounds would benefit from this annual celebration.

CREATE A MENU FROM A LOCAL FARMERS' MARKET

Most of the larger towns in Montana host a farmers market of some kind, and often two or three. When it comes time to plan the evening meal, consider a market-themed family outing. The food will be guaranteed farm-to-table, and your money will go directly to support another family's livelihood.

In Missoula, you've got your Clark Fork River Market and the Missoula Farmers' Market on the north end of Higgins Avenue.

The Bozeman Farmers' Market is on Tuesdays in Lindley Park while the Gallatin Valley Farmers' Market occurs every summer Saturday at the fairgrounds. Google both events for cancellations and schedule variations.

A couple hours down the Interstate, Billings has the Yellowstone Valley Farmers' Market (billed as the largest in Montana) on Saturdays from mid-July to early October. They're at the intersection of 2nd Avenue North and North Broadway downtown. The Gardeners' Market at South Park, on the corner of South 28th and 7th

Avenue South, runs from the second week of June through the first week in October.

Helena has the Capitol Square Farmer's Market as well as the Farmers' Market on Fuller Street.

Kid Friendly ★★★★★

Most kids don't enjoy shopping for food, but most kids also need to know where their food comes from. Drag them along and give them a pedantic lecture about how most everything we eat comes at the expense of someone else's labor.

HUTTERITES

MONTANA HAS roughly fifty Hutterite colonies scattered around the state, with a total population of around five thousand. Communal farms, they'll often have a roadside sign advertising fresh eggs, pork, vegetables, or poultry for sale. They don't give tours but you can stop by to load up on what's missing in your fridge. Take the opportunity to ask a polite question or two.

mahalie stackpole

A German-speaking Anabaptist sect, the first Hutterite colony in Montana was established near Lewistown in 1912. Wary of outside interaction, these colonies have nevertheless had an outsized impact on the state's economy. A 2019 university study found that the state's Hutterite communities contribute more than $365 million in annual spending for Montana.

WHITEWATER RAFT OR KAYAK

There are certain very touristy things in Montana we would never recommend you try (we'd rather punch ourselves in the nose than go zip lining, for instance), but whitewater rafting with a commercial outfitter seems kind of like the ideal space-filler for a hot August afternoon. You get the float experience and, if you're inclined, you get the swimming experience. You can paddle with a group, and of course you get the momentary, roller-coaster thrill of the whitewater.

In Bozeman, the commercial groups gravitate toward either the Gallatin River or the Madison River through Beartrap Canyon. Depending on flows, both can be white-knuckle floats. House Rock on the Gallatin seems to cause one or two fatalities a year, and the Kitchen Sink through the Beartrap is a pretty legit Class 4, nearly Class 5. Over the hill south of Livingston, the Yellowstone through Yankee Jim is a fun float as well.

Thirty-five miles out of Missoula, you can float Alberton Gorge on the Clark Fork, either half day or full days. There's also the Blackfoot River an hour or so away.

If you have time, the Middle Fork and North Fork of the Flathead are both world-class floats, not necessarily for the whitewater so much as the overall, Glacier-but-not-quite-Glacier experience. The Middle Fork in particular, running as it does through the middle of the Bob Marshall

Wilderness (you start out by flying into a small air strip in the middle of the Bob), is a bucket-list experience. Fishing while you float, and not even trying too hard, you might catch thirty or forty cutthroats a day. We went with Glacier Raft Company twenty years ago and had the time of our lives.

Kid Friendly

Older kids who are comfortable in the water will likely talk about a good whitewater trip for weeks afterward. Be cautious about younger kids, though. Even using a commercial outfitter, a whitewater float can be quite dangerous.

Rafters on the Gallatin River south of Bozeman

FORT BENTON

It would be hard to find more Western history packed into one small town than in Fort Benton. Front Street in particular—that part of town running next to the Missouri—has seen some times. Established as a fur-trapping outpost in 1846, by the early 1860s Fort Benton was the steamboat terminus on the Missouri River. During the early gold rush years, if you were in Montana, you likely traveled through Fort Benton. These days, walking down Front Street, you'll see interpretive signs for the Bloodiest Block in the West and for the first bridge across the Missouri in Montana. You'll see statues for Lewis and Clark and for Shep, the dog that famously (and heartbreakingly) kept waiting at the train station for its late owner. There's also a bronze bust of Thomas Meagher, a territorial governor who disappeared into the river on this location in 1867 (murder or suicide, it's still debated).

FURTHER SUGGESTIONS FOR SUMMER

Ski Beartooth Basin

For the hardcore downhill skiers, it's possible to carve some unearned turns in June or even July. At the top of the Beartooth Pass above Red Lodge, there's an unlikely ski lift. Go to beartoothbasin.com.

Grizzly Discovery Center

It's a rare trip to Yellowstone Park that lets you catch a glimpse of a grizzly or a wolf. Coming out of the Park through West Yellowstone, give yourself a consolation prize and visit the Grizzly Discovery Center. They also have otters, hawks, and eagles.

Raptor Center

In Bozeman, the Montana Raptor Conservation Center has been saving raptors since 1988. They offer outreach programs and demonstration events in the summer.

Pick Some Huckleberries

Not unlike morel mushrooms, picking hucks in Montana is a seasonal, near-sacred event. Productive patches are hard to come by and jealously guarded. Start out by hiking three or four miles up a public trail and pay attention to the shrubs.

FALL

Coming out of a hot Montana summer, the shorter days and cooler nights of autumn are a relief. If you're any sort of a hunter or a fisherman, this is the finest time of year. September, October, and November are why you live here. Bulls bugle, brown trout kick up their redds, and geese start heading south in high-altitude vees. Dust off your decoys, consider tying some streamers, and start shooting your bow in the backyard like you mean it.

For campers and hikers, the parks are officially transitioning into shoulder season. Fair warning, though: Once you've hung out in Yellowstone or Glacier in late September or October, you'll have a hard time settling for a summer trip.

Looking ahead to the long tunnel of winter, the fall weekends will sustain you. You only get so many in a lifetime. Plan accordingly.

33

HEAR A BULL ELK BUGLE

For certain key species in Montana—biologists call them charismatic megafauna—autumn is the time for love, for skirt chasing, for frenetically passing their genes on to the next generation. In November, mule deer and whitetail bucks see their necks swell up past the jawline; in late August, antelope bucks gather their does into a harem, and in September bull elk start calling out to competitors. If you've lived in Montana for any time at all, the sound of an elk bugle is an immediate evocation of the best time of year.

> **Factoid**
>
> The National Bison Range was established in 1908 by Teddy Roosevelt. In 2020, Congress ordered the lands to be held in trust for the Confederated Salish and Kootenai tribes.

Avid bowhunters will walks for miles in the backcountry trying to get close to a bull. You bring your own bugle and stand on a high point. Blow out a whistle, and then stand listening. If you get a response, you plan your morning hunt accordingly. If you don't get a response, you move on to the next overlook. Some bulls, particularly when they're especially hot and bothered, will come into a bugling hunter not unlike a turkey coming into a gobble. There's no greater thrill in the world.

Folks who aren't bowhunters, however, can still find the sound of a bugling bull. Try Mammoth, on the north end

The larger bull elk will typically have a deeper, hoarser bugle than the shrill, one-or-two-note whistle that comes from younger bulls.

Rutting bull elk like to scrape at brush and tree saplings with their antlers, sometimes destroying the vegetation.

of Yellowstone. There will likely be a bull or two right in town. In Western Montana, you can travel to the 18,800-acre National Bison Range. In Eastern Montana, consider spending an evening at the Slippery Ann Game Preserve on the Missouri River, just west of Fort Peck Lake. (You'll be competing with a platoon-sized group of wildlife photographers, but it's still worthwhile.) There's a campground, but it will be full. Stay in Lewistown or maybe Malta.

Like a number of other seasonal activities in Montana, the elk bugling will really only be an excuse to get out, to try your hand at some other local activities. While you're in Lewistown, consider fishing Big Spring Creek. It's a little tricky if you don't know the water, so hire a guide if you can afford it. Everybody but me has had a great day fishing there.

While you're hanging out next to the Missouri, rig up some worms on a bobber and toss it out there, see what you can drag back to shore. The warmwater fishing in Montana is often overshadowed by the trout fishing, but the Missouri has world-class fishing for smallmouth bass, catfish, walleye, even the occasional northern pike.

> **HELPFUL TIP**
>
> In many of the places where you can expect to hear an elk bugle (Yellowstone National Park, the National Bison Range), there are some very specific laws regarding harassment of wildlife. Research before you go. It might save you from some uncomfortable conversations with law enforcement.

By late September, some bull elk will have broken the tips off their antlers, fighting other bulls.

Something to keep in mind: Inflatable kayaks are quite affordable these days. Throw one of those bad boys into the back of your truck and scoot across to the other side of the river, away from the competition.

Kid Friendly

If you build in some kid-approved side trips, this one has all sorts of family friendly potential. There's nothing quite like planning a trip to hear an elk bugle, and then actually making it happen.

34

TAKE A JAW-DROPPING SCENIC DRIVE

In Montana, it's pretty much impossible to drive more than an hour in one direction without taking in some scenery. You're going to be either in the mountains or on the prairie. There's you and the road and the sky. The Missoula poet Richard Hugo said something about how your car has never found so forward a gear.

These days, of course, our cars are mostly utilitarian objects. So long as they work, we tend to forget about them. But it didn't always used to be this way. Remember Sunday family drives? They were occasions. A way for a family to spend unproductive time together without necessarily having to look each other in the eye. Maybe we can get there again.

South of Red Lodge, try the Beartooth Highway to Cooke City. It plateaus out at just under eleven thousand feet. The road from Cooke into Yellowstone is, at this moment, closed for flood repairs. Google before you go.

South of Missoula, try the Skalkaho Highway between Hamilton and Philipsburg via the Sapphires. It tops out at not quite eight thousand feet,

The beauty in Eastern Montana is hard to capture in a camera sensor.

Looking down on Twin Lakes from the road over Beartooth Pass

and the curves aren't for the car-sick inclined, but the views will knock you out. And at the end of it, you're rewarded with Philipsburg and The Sweet Palace candy store.

In the northwest, there's the Lake Koocanusa Scenic Byway, and in Eastern Montana, the Big Sky Byway, according to the excellent visitmt.com website, follows "a section of the historic Regina-Yellowstone (R-Y) Trail, which tourists from Canada used to reach Yellowstone National Park."

Kid Friendly

If you have kids strapped into a car seat or arguing in the back seat, it's probably a good idea to build some incentives into your scenic drive. Promise them ice cream at the end of the road, or a visit to the Philipsburg candy store (below).

The Sweet Palace in Philipsburg has been a draw for twenty-five years. They're closed on Saturdays, though.

WORK MONTANA'S STREAM ACCESS LAW

As opposed to most other western states, Montana has a generous (and often-attacked) stream access law. In a nutshell, the waterways are considered public property, up to the high water mark. If you can access a stream, you can walk up or down it to fish. This is of enormous benefit to the public, both to residents as well as to the average-Joe nonresident fisherman. In Wyoming, by contrast, landowners own the stream beds that run through their property, meaning that while you might be able to float over a fishery, you can't step on it. For the general public, there's effectively no private-property wade fishing in Wyoming. In Montana, we have it better.

It goes back to the late seventies and early eighties. A Butte-based grassroots organization called the Montana Stream Access Coalition took a landowner to court, resulting, in 1984, with a state Supreme Court ruling that institutionalized sportsman's access to the state's waterways. These laws have been challenged a number of times since, typically by landowners who, naturally enough, I suppose, come to resent the fact that while they pay taxes on a particular piece of ground, and while they may have invested in stream improvements (maybe they fenced off some riverbank, maybe they pulled the cows off their place), it's possible, even likely, that the public will see the benefit of their efforts without any sort of acknowledgment from the state.

Two sides to every pancake. Increasingly, this contrast between private property rights and public access (you see it most vividly in conflicts surrounding publicly owned wildlife on private property) has come to define the West. There are overtones of social stratification and one-percenters vs. the rest of us.

But what this means for the average Montana fisherman, for the nine-to-fiver taking off a little early in order to wet a fly, or for the college kid passing through on spring break, is that some outstanding fly fishing is available for those who don't mind a hike inside the high water mark. As long as you're walking within the stream bed, you're probably legal. This doesn't give you a free pass to be inconsiderate, though. Don't leave trash, and be cautious about spreading invasives.

> **HELPFUL TIP**
>
> As you fish small streams, keep an eye out for spawning redds. These are the stretches of gravel, often in some of the shallower water, wherein trout have maneuvered a place to lay their eggs. Rainbows and cutthroat spawn in the spring, brown trout spawn in the fall. If you see redds or actively spawning trout, leave them alone. They need room to do their thing.

Kid Friendly

Most kids won't dig the effort it takes to fish a small stream—the ankle-twisting hikes up and down gravel bars, the frustrating ducks through willow flats. If you can get them to tag along, though, and when they hook onto that lunker, just watch them grin.

36

DROP IN ON A SMALLER MUSEUM

When it comes to museums, Montana really does have an embarrassment of riches. There's the Museum of the Rockies in Bozeman and the Montana Historical Society in Helena, as well as dozens of smaller museums, each one invested with the passions of their local supporters. In Missoula, for instance, there's the Rocky Mountain Elk Foundation. An admirable organization with an unfortunate history of incompetent leadership, they have a display area that's worth a few minutes of your time. If you have an appreciation for artful taxidermy, some of the elk mounts are worth the trip.

Speaking of taxidermy, if you're north of Great Falls, take a side trip to check out the Chinook Wildlife Museum. Chinook, like most of the towns on the Hi-Line (that stretch of Highway 2 from Shelby to Glasgow), has been having a rough go of it lately—a dwindling tax base and many of the youngsters with ambition heading to brighter

Next door to the Wildlife Museum in Chinook, the Blaine County Museum offers exhibits on the Bear Paw Battlefield as well as some exceptional Charlie Russell letters.

The wildlife museum in Chinook is supported in large part by community donations and fundraisers.

lights and bigger cities—Chinook nevertheless decided to do something about it. A small group of town fathers got together and created a tourist attraction—a wildlife museum that features life-sized dioramas with hand-painted backgrounds and ambient soundtracks. Informational signs and a gift shop. The whole thing is supported by community donations.

It's an artful and compelling set of exhibits, but even more, it's an admirable example of what can be accomplished when a town collectively sets its shoulder to a common wheel.

Next door, the Blaine County Museum is one of the finer county museums in Montana. If you're traveling to the Bear Paw Battlefield to the south, stop there first.

Kid Friendly

The Chinook Wildlife Museum was created for families. Careful about trip planning, though. There aren't many places to stay or eat on the Hi-Line. Pack a cooler and plan out your motels.

37

PADDLE A CANOE TRAIL

In our twenties and thirties, we pulled a driftboat around Montana. A beat up old Clacka, cracked on the gunnels and scratched everywhere it could be scratched, it was almost indestructible. If you know what you're doing, you can float pretty much anywhere in Montana with a good driftboat, up to and including some lower-digit whitewater. In our forties, though, tired of pulling a trailer and having caught all the fish we really needed to catch, we switched to a family canoe. An Old Town three-seater that straps, without too much trouble, on top of our pickup.

As opposed to drift boats, however, you need to be a bit pickier about what sort of water you choose for your canoe. Unless you're familiar with a given stretch of river, maybe you rely on somebody else's suggestions. Outside of Bozeman, for instance, the Jefferson River Canoe Trail, established by the Jefferson River Chapter of the Lewis & Clark Trail Heritage Foundation, "retraces by water an essential segment of the Lewis & Clark National Historic Trail along the entire length of the Jefferson River in southwest Montana." Their maps offer suggested primitive campsites along the way, either on BLM or within the high water mark, as allowed by Montana's

Karen Kenyon

The Clearwater River Canoe Trail north of Seeley Lake (above) flows into the lake through a carpet of lily pads (left).

stream access laws.

North of Seeley, a very nice, very calm (a little too calm, honestly) stretch of the Clearwater flows into Seeley Lake. When we paddled this canoe trail a few years ago, we were briefly confused by the braided stream, but then were rewarded at the end of the float by paddling through constellations of lily pads at the entrance to the lake proper.

Kid Friendly ★★★★☆

Give a kid their own oar and watch them happily flail around.

THE RINGING ROCKS

East of Butte, north of I-90, not far from the little town of Whitehall (it shows up on Google maps), at the end of one of those gravel roads that makes you wonder if you're *ever* going to get there, you'll find a pile of boulders. A good portion of these rocks give off a distinct chime when you hit them with a hammer. This isn't a state park, although maybe it should be. When we visited, there were a few extra hammers hanging on a board for visitors to try. The kids will enjoy scrambling up and down the boulders, hitting various rocks to explore the tones. The last little bit of the road is quite rough, though. A high-clearance vehicle would be a good idea.

38

BAG SOME STATE PARKS

There are fifty-five state parks in Montana, scattered here and there around the state. You've got your picnic tables beside Flathead Lake and you've got your hikes through eroded badlands. In terms of recreational opportunities, the state parks pretty much run the gamut.

We like our history in Montana, and that's reflected in the number of sites designated as state parks. According to Montana's Fish, Wildlife, and Parks, the state park system "provides stewardship for more than 350 historic and archaeological sites, including seven National Historic Landmarks, and 11 sites currently listed in the National Register of Historic Places." Among these notable historical sites is the Anaconda Smoke Stack State Park, a viewing area with interpretive signs, describing the size and importance of the stack. At 585 feet tall and built in 1919, it's one of the tallest freestanding brick structures in the world. It was decommissioned in

The smokestack in Anaconda, having served as the smelter for Butte's mines before being decommissioned, is taller than the Washington Monument.

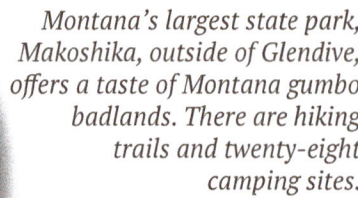

Montana's largest state park, Makoshika, outside of Glendive, offers a taste of Montana gumbo badlands. There are hiking trails and twenty-eight camping sites.

1980. Other historic state parks include ghost towns (Granite, Bannack, Elkhorn), lakes and reservoirs, and a battlefield (Rosebud Battlefield).

Montana's relationship with Native Americans, and that history (complicated, heartbreaking, so often less than admirable), is also represented by our state parks. The First People's Buffalo Jump State Park outside of Great Falls is a two-thousand-acre preserve that draws attention to one of the most significant buffalo jump sites in the nation. A six thousand square foot interpretive center helps provide context and history. The Madison Buffalo Jump west of Bozeman is an excellent place to take a day hike. There's a kiosk at the end of a short hike, and if you have more time and are capable, a longer hike gives you some great views from the top of the buffalo jump. On both sites, be wary of rattlesnakes and, if you're going to be outside on a warm day, bring drinking water for the hike.

Chief Plenty Coups State Park, about forty minutes south of Billings, commemorates the last traditional chief of the Crow Nation. The 195 acres of sacred spring, log home, and farmstead go back to a 320-acre parcel of land given to Chief Plenty Coups in 1884 through the Federal Indian Allotment Act.

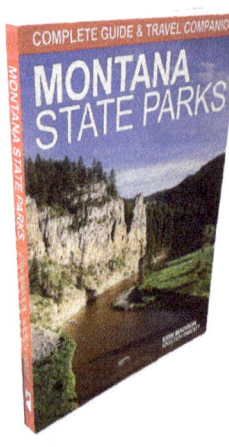

Montana State Parks, *by Erin Madison and Kristen Inbody, is a valuable resource.*

Plenty Coups, or Aleek-chea-ahoosh ("Many Achievements"), was recognized for his leadership in both wartime and peacetime. According to the state parks website, visitors should "plan at least an hour to walk the grounds and browse through the Visitor Center that commemorates the life of this remarkable man and his efforts to lead his people into bridging the gap between two cultures." There is a 3/4-mile trail around the park next to Pryor Creek, along with some picnic tables. The park is day use only.

Kid Friendly

A state-park themed excursion can provide structure on an outing that might otherwise seem capricious and flippant. Kids like structure, right?

MONTANA LICENSE PLATES

SOME OF THE LICENSE plates you see in Montana are fundraising mechanisms. Beginning in 2001, if you were a nonprofit, advocacy group, or educational institute, you could submit your own license plate design and offer it to the public as a way to raise money. The numbers on these plates have their own system, unrelated to the population at large. Prior to this system, however, Montana plates all began with a one- or two-digit number. These numbers were, and are, county designations. When the system began in 1926, they referenced the counties by their population as of 1914. Silver Bow County, with the mining city of Butte, was then the most populous county in the state. Butte license plates still start with the number 1.

A variety of wildlife can be found across Montana's state parks, including bighorn sheep on Wild Horse Island. In the middle of Flathead Lake, Wild Horse can be difficult to access (you'll need to borrow or hire a motor boat) and there are very few improvements, but the island makes for an adventurous day trip.

39

BEND A KNEE TO LEWIS AND CLARK

Lewis and Clark are to Montana what Mickey Mouse is to Disneyland, what Iron Man is to Marvel, what Harry Potter is to Hogwarts. In order to fully get a grip on the Rocky Mountain West, you need to understand the Corps of Discovery.

Meriwether Lewis, William Clark, and thirty-some other guys famously went up the Missouri River in 1803, at the request of President Thomas Jefferson, to explore and map the newly acquired Louisiana Purchase and try to find a navigable route to the Pacific. They returned in 1806. Coming and going, they spent more time in what would become the state of Montana than any other region.

> **Factoid**
>
> Lewis and Clark's Shoshone guide, Sacajawea, as famous as she is, remains something of a mystery. No one really knows what she looked like, for instance. Somewhat inexplicably, Lewis and Clark failed to bring an artist along on their expedition.

Montana is well aware of this social and cultural significance, and the state has done its best to live up to it. There are countless little brown-and-white signs scattered hither and yon, letting you know that you're on the Lewis and Clark trail. There is also the Travelers' Rest State Park south of Lolo, the Missouri Headwaters State Park outside Three

The interpretive center in Great Falls gives visitors a sense for the heroic effort it took for Lewis and Clark to portage the falls of the Missouri River.

Forks, Beaverhead Rock and Clark's Lookout State Parks in Beaverhead County, Tower Rock State Park in Cascade County, and more interpretive signs scattered around than you can shake a hiking stick at. Lost Pass Trail Summit in Ravalli County, Lolo Hot Springs in Missoula County, and Russell Memorial Gates Fishing Access Campground in Missoula County all have interpretive signs.

In Great Falls, you should stop at the Lewis and Clark National Historic Trail Interpretive Center on Giant Springs Road. The self-described centerpiece of the museum is a two-story diorama "illustrating the portage of the Missouri River's five great falls."

Pompey's Pillar preserves the only extant physical evidence of the Lewis and Clark expedition.

But perhaps the crown jewel of the Lewis and Clark experience in Montana is Pompey's Pillar National Monument on the Yellowstone River, twenty-five miles east of Billings off exit 23 on Interstate 94. A large sandstone outcropping above a relatively shallow stretch of the river (creating a natural ford), the pillar has attracted all sorts of engravings over the years, including the only surviving physical evidence of the Lewis and Clark expedition, William Clark's signature, now under protective glass.

Kid Friendly

History is tricky with most kids, but if you present it to them as an ongoing narrative, potentially with questions that need answered, you might hook them in.

The Lewis and Clark Memorial in Fort Benton by sculptor Bob Scriver commemorates the nine days the Corps of Discovery spent at the confluence of the Marias and Missouri Rivers.

40

DIP INTO ESSENTIAL MONTANA BOOKS, STREAMSIDE

When it comes to good writing, and for whatever reason, Montana has been gifted with an embarrassment of riches. A. B. Guthrie, Jr.'s monumental novel *The Big Sky* not only gave us the first artful look at a mountain man (Boone Caudill), it also gave us the state's nickname. Guthrie is a great place to start, but it's only the first domino in one of those gymnasium-filling, Guinness world-record-breaking arrangement of dominoes.

Pick a nice fall day in late September or early October, pack a lunch and a lawn chair, and walk upstream from a good access point. You just need to get far enough away from the road to mute the traffic noise. Bonus points if you have a dog, maybe a Lab. Look up from the page now and then to go bemused at your pup's joy as it investigates various smells. Insist that the kids leave their devices in the car. After the initial, obligatory twenty minutes of complaining, they'll start building sand castles and arranging rocks, splashing at

The poet Richard Hugo, forty years after his passing, remains an essential part of Montana's literary heritage.

the water with sticks, falling in, crying, drying off, then jumping in intentionally.

Once you've read *The Big Sky*, try something by James Welch. Maybe *Winter in the Blood* or *Fool's Crow*. A member of the Blackfeet tribe, few writers have written about the Native American experience as artfully as Welch. If you have any taste for poetry at all, try Richard Hugo's selected poems (Hugo was Welch's mentor) or maybe *The Shape of the Journey*, collected poems by Jim Harrison. Harrison was a seasonal resident of Montana.

If non-fiction is more your bag, try *Fifty-Six Counties* by Russell Rowland or *Montana: Then and Now* by Aaron Parrett, both of them big-picture overviews of our state. William Kittredge's essays are insightful and artful glimpses into the region, while Norman Maclean's *A River Runs Through It* is always worth a revisit. As a friend on Facebook put it, it's the book that launched a thousand drift boats. Thomas McGuane has been living and writing in Montana since the late 1960s, producing personal essays, short stories, and novels. Maybe start with his short story collection, *Cloudbursts*, then go on to his sporting

essays, *The Longest Silence*. Ivan Doig wrote a whole passel of fantastic novels set in Montana, but the entry point is probably his memoir, *This House of Sky*. Read it, and then take a road trip to Ringling and White Sulphur Springs to eyeball the country that nurtured him.

In Bozeman, Mark Sullivan has gone from writing thrillers to historical nonfiction. His two bestsellers, *Beneath a Scarlet Sky* and *The Last Green Valley*, have established him as one of the most widely read authors in the Rocky Mountain West. Up in Malta, B.J. Daniels writes some smashing cowboy-centric romance novels.

> **HELPFUL TIP**
>
> There are some fantastic independent bookstores in Montana, all of them staffed by readers who know the region's literature front to back. When you buy a book from the Country Bookshelf in Bozeman, Fact and Fiction in Missoula, Elk River Books in Livingston, This House of Books in Billings, or any of the other regional indys, you are not only paying for the expertise of a recommendation, you are supporting the livelihoods of friends and neighbors.

The list of top-shelf Montana writers just goes on and on. Jamie Harrison, Paul Zarzyski, Debra Magpie Earling, David James Duncan, Annick Smith, Mary Clearman Blew, Pete Fromm, Rick Bass, James Lee Burke, Kevin Canty, Deirdre McNamer, Tami Haaland, Gwen Florio, Craig Lancaster…if you just make any sort of effort at all, there is something here for pretty much any taste or sensibility.

They are all best read, however, with running water as the soundtrack.

Kid Friendly

In our opinion, there's no such thing as a kid who doesn't like to read. There are only kids who haven't yet found their favorite books. Start with comics and graphic novels, then move on.

41

CATCH THE CAT-GRIZ FOOTBALL GAME

There are two Division I colleges in Montana: The University of Montana in Missoula (the Grizzlies), and Montana State University in Bozeman (the Bobcats). As you can imagine, there's a *liiiittle* bit of a rivalry between the two.

It's a rivalry that extends to pretty much every interaction between the two colleges, but it really heats up for the annual football game. Called the Brawl of the Wild by the marketing folks, or just Cat-Griz by the locals, the rivalry goes back to 1897. As of this writing, there have been over 120 meetings between the two football teams.

Held during the final week of regular play in either Missoula or Bozeman (it alternates, year to year) Cat-Griz tickets are tough to come by. But you don't need to be in the stadium to get a sense for the rivalry. The tailgating is top shelf, and there's always a downtown bar that will have the enthusiasm spilling out into the street.

Kid Friendly

Depends on the kid, of course, and their enthusiasm for sports.

42

BIRD HUNT ON THE AMERICAN PRAIRIE

The American Prairie (formerly American Prairie Reserve) is an improbably ambitious (and controversial) ongoing conservation project in Northeastern Montana. With the long-term goal, a few generations down the line, of creating the first privately-held grasslands National Park in North America, the Prairie uses donations to buy ranches and roll them over into the public commons. They've reintroduced bison, they encourage prairie dogs, and they discourage predator hunting. They wouldn't mind it if grizzlies and wolves started showing up again. While the rest of the world is getting paved over in asphalt, the Prairie's goal is to ultimately reproduce the same habitat that greeted Lewis and Clark when they pulled their boats up the river some 220 years ago.

There's a campaign in Eastern Montana against the Prairie, however. You'll see the signs occasionally: "Save the Cowboy. Stop the American Prairie Reserve." It's unclear to us how stopping the Prairie would save the cowboy, but folks are free to believe what they like. The controversy, as far as we can tell, largely revolves around the way in which the Prairie is buying range ground and taking it out of traditional production. It's perhaps seen as a commentary on an established way of life. The locals don't dig the bison too much, either.

Sharptail grouse are native to much of the habitat preserved by American Prairie.

Among the improvements taken on by the Prairie, they have refurbished a homestead-era schoolhouse.

It's no doubt a hard thing, to have a nonprofit, mostly supported by wealthy out-of-staters, displace your neighbors, but we stand by a landowner's right to do what they want with their own property, particularly if it adds to the public good.

In any case, the Prairie considers itself public ground. As a member of the public, you are welcomed to hike and camp on their property. They also participate in Montana's block management program. As a hunter, you contact the Prairie and tell them where and when you would like to hunt, then sign your name on a register. In return for offering the public access, the Prairie then receives a modest stipend from the state. With the goal of rebuilding the flora and fauna toward its original condition, they discourage certain types of hunting and encourage others. Even if they don't allow access for, say, elk hunting, they will allow you to drive through in order to access adjacent public ground.

As of this writing, the Prairie has opened more than ninety thousand acres of habitat to bird hunting. Or if bird hunting isn't your bag, it's worth the drive (five or six hours from Bozeman) to simply hike through the Prairie. Photograph the bison and prairie dogs. Have a campfire under more stars than you thought possible. There's an improved campsite with tent platforms at their Sun Prairie property, but you're welcome to throw out a tent pretty much anywhere. There's also a hut-to-hut trail system.

The public campground at Sun Prairie offers elevated tent platforms, creating stable and comfortable sleeping areas.

The primary motivation behind the American Prairie, we believe, is generosity. For the major donors, there's no doubt some ego gratification involved, but for the most part, it's an attempt to create something lasting that will be of benefit to others. It's an attempt to preserve a modest corner of an under-appreciated ecosystem. And while we are sympathetic with the localized opposition, we feel that the larger benefits far outweigh any negatives.

Kid Friendly

The experiences offered by American Prairie are, in the context of most Montana vacations, exceptional and unusual. Getting to the Prairie from Missoula, Bozeman, or even Billings means a lot of time in the car, but your kids will come back with some great stories.

WHITE CLIFFS OF THE MISSOURI

ONE OF THE BEST multi-day float trips in Montana is through the Upper Missouri River National Monument past the White Cliffs of the Missouri. Made of Virgelle sandstone, the cliffs have appeared in any number of famous paintings and photographs. Meriwether Lewis wrote, "So perfect indeed are those walls that I should have thought that nature had attempted here to rival the human art of masonry..." It's a three- or four-day float from Coal Banks Landing to the Judith River takeout. There are no amenities, so you have to bring everything with you, including drinking water, food, and bug spray. Lots of bug spray. Watch out for rattlesnakes, and anticipate dodging some free-range cattle as well. We love DIY multi-day excursions but, in this case, you may want to consider hiring an outfitter. Start looking in Fort Benton.

FURTHER SUGGESTIONS FOR FALL

Walk Across the Swinging Bridge at Kootenai Falls

With original construction dating back to 1939, the Swinging Bridge over the Kootenai (Northwestern Montana), offers unusual views of the river, and makes for a nice reason to just take a drive.

Get Confused in a Hay or Corn Maze

A quick Google shows at least seven different substantial corn and hay mazes around Montana. Our neighborhood hay maze in Bozeman is on Valley Center Road.

Visit the Daly Mansion in the Bitterroot

Marcus Daly was one of Montana's original "copper kings." He made his money in Butte, then set up shop in the Bitterroot. Forty-seven acres of grounds and 24,000 square feet of mansion offer a glimpse into the plutocrats of the previous century.

Road Trip to the Bair Museum

Home to one of the wealthiest and historically more significant families in Montana, the Charles M. Bair home is now a period showroom and art museum in Martinsdale. They're open every day in the summer, and Wednesday through Sunday in September and October.

Great Montana Weekends 157

WINTER

Winter in Montana is all about challenges and rewards. In order to stay sane during the longer nights and shorter days, through the season of snow tires and chains, frozen pipes and cold toes, you need to get outside. You *need* to get outside. It just takes a little more effort, a little more creativity, than it might in the warmer months.

Among the many arguments for winter, this is the season that lets you get a sense for who your friends really are. Not only who's going to pull you out of the ditch, but who's going to be willing to crawl out of bed to go skiing, maybe snowshoeing or ice fishing or snowmobiling. Who's going to have the energy and emotional wherewithal to help you jump-start an expedition?

When you have to stay inside, just *have* to, this is also the perfect time of year to catch up on your museums.

43

SKI A CROSS-COUNTRY RESORT

If you're a fitness enthusiast, cross-country skiing is the bomb. It's a full-body workout that gets you out of the house and into the sunlight during the dreariest part of the year. And even if you'd just kind of like to get back in some kind of shape maybe someday, the solitude and freedom of cross-country skiing is a considerable draw. In the middle of winter, this is how you get out in the woods.

But if you're casual about it, or if you're traveling, the barriers to entry can be considerable. Where do you go? How do you proceed safely? And most of all where do you find your equipment?

There are a handful of commercial cross-country ski trail systems scattered around Montana, and some of them offer ski rentals. Access is often free, or at least affordable. Trail systems are groomed and well maintained. If ski rentals aren't available close to the trails themselves, call around to the local ski shops. Somebody is likely to rent.

Outside of Bozeman, just past Bridger Bowl, we're big fans of Crosscut. With more than 45 km of trails, you can skate ski or go the classic route. Rentals are available on site,

Crosscut Mountain offers ski rentals on site—a considerable convenience for most families.

and dogs are allowed in the afternoons three days a week.

Outside of Big Sky, there's Lone Mountain Ranch—nice, but limited to guests of the resort. Around Red Lodge, the Red Lodge Nordic Center sponsors grooming of more than 15 km of trails. If you're around Whitefish, Google the Glacier Nordic Center, and if you're in Great Falls, consider Silver Crest Trails around Neihardt. Closer to Missoula the Seeley Lake Nordic Ski Club maintains a fantastic series of trails.

Kid Friendly ★★★★☆

Not unlike hiking, some kids might need an incentive to see the value in cross-country skiing. Throw in hot chocolate and a pair of binoculars for birds and squirrels.

YELLOWSTONE PARK CROSS-COUNTRY SKIING

Yellowstone has some of the coolest cross-country skiing in the country. From Montana, most skiing happens off the only road in the park to stay open year-round: Highway 212 between Mammoth and Cooke City. Bad news? No dogs allowed. If you're not too concerned about bringing your pup along, however, the skiing is well worth a pilgrimage. The road winds through the Lamar Valley, which always offers primo wildlife viewing. Out of Mammoth, at the end of Highway 89, there's a maintained trail loop that winds through a few hot springs. The loop is accessible and a good length for beginners. Be careful, though. Bears are hibernating but there are still bison around. Keep your distance. There's also an admission fee. If you think you'll go more than once, buy an annual pass.

CAST AND BLAST ON THE BIGHORN

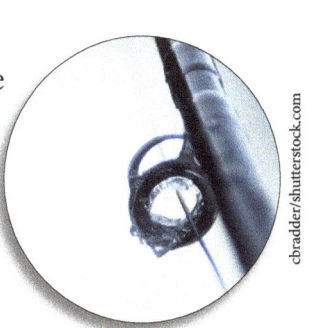

Like a number of other tailwaters, the Bighorn River below Yellowtail Reservoir maintains a steady, year-round, trout-friendly temperature. This means that in the late fall and winter, the fish remain active and hungry. Ducks and geese are also drawn to the open water.

For the purposes of regulatory oversight, Montana distinguishes between two separate waterfowl areas. There's the Pacific Flyway and the Central Flyway. There are currently split seasons in each, and seasonal variations with regard to ducks versus geese. (It's complicated enough to that you need to keep tabs, year to year.)

If you're inclined to have a do-it-yourself adventure, find a buddy with a drift boat and throw in some decoys, grab your fly rod and make sure you're loaded up on streamers. Bundle up and bring some handwarmers, maybe a flask. Research the regs. For a certain, self-flagellating mindset, there are few things so enjoyable as a morning spent dredging streamers before pulling into a backwater to call in some geese.

Kid Friendly

This one's for the grownups.

HIKE UP THE BEAR TRAP TO FISH THE MADISON

One of the more popular hiking trails outside of Bozeman is into Bear Trap Canyon. Roughly forty-five minutes from Bozeman, this trail is popular with dog walkers, trail runners, picnickers, bird watchers… anyone who needs a convenient break from the disheartening bustle of Bozeman.

Among fly-fishers, the Bear Trap is well known for its winter fishing. Given the heat sink of Ennis Lake just upstream, the water stays open year around, and is actually better fishing on a cloudy, blustery winter afternoon than in the heat of the summer. The hiking also tends to winnow out some of the less fit or less enthusiastic fishermen. You're still going to have some competition, but it's probably not going to be as noticeable as it would be just a mile or two downstream.

> **Factoid**
>
> *In the mid-1990s, whirling disease appeared in the Madison River. At one time, it may have been responsible for killing off as much as 90 percent of the Madison's rainbows. Thanks to good conservation practices and stream-flow controls, the fishery has since experienced a dramatic recovery.*

Nicely, one of the cool things about the Bear Trap is that the quality of fishing tends to reward hard work. The first few patches of boulders you come to are going to yield

Fishing in the Bear Trap tends to be better in January and February than it is in August.

a few fish, but the further up you go, the better the fishing is likely going to get. Bring a lunch and some hand warmers. Decide whether to hike in your waders or carry a backpack. Plan on a double-nymph rig to start out. If you start seeing rises, throw on a tiny little midge.

Kid Friendly

Depending on the age and temperament of your kids, the combination of hiking and cold weather may be whine-inducing.

46

FISH SOME HARD WATER

We haven't ice fished as much since we cut back on the drinking (ice fishing makes it a little too easy to rationalize peppermint schnapps with the hot chocolate), but for an enthusiastic contingent of Montana sportsmen and women, there is just as much skill, just as much brio and talent, involved in ice fishing as there is in slinging around any sort of fancy-pantsy fly rod. For this rare breed, ice fishing isn't just a way to fill in the months between December and April. It's not a means to an end—it *is* the end. So to speak.

Entry level ice fishing, you walk out onto the ice to a likely spot, dragging a sled that holds your auger or spud, an ice-fishing rod or two, maybe a thermos of hot chocolate. Augur up some shavings. Turn a bucket upside down beside the hole. Thread on a bullhead if you're in Eastern Montana, maybe some maggots if you're in the Western part of the state, and drop down your line.

When we fished for Kokanee on Georgetown Lake, we were told the appropriate depth was eight or ten feet down. Pinch a bobber on the line and set it atop the pile of ice shavings. Make sure your reel isn't locked. Then wait. And wait. Maybe take a picture

Georgetown Lake, above and right, offers some excellent ice fishing.

with your phone. Wonder why it doesn't look like *Field and Stream*. If you have a cell signal, try to get the scores. Jig a few times up and down. Every once in a while, you'll feel a tug and pull something surprising out into the light.

Ice fishing regulations, like all FWP regs, can be quite complicated, varying region to region and even lake to lake. Research it before you go in order to avoid having one of those uncomfortable conversations with a friendly game warden.

Kid Friendly

We've heard that some kids like sitting out on an icy lake in the middle of the winter. We haven't met those kids, however.

47

CHECK OUT THE MUSEUM OF THE ROCKIES

In Montana's mud season, if you're in or around Bozeman, there are few better ways to spend an afternoon than at the Museum of the Rockies (MoR).

Located on the south side of town, just down Kagy from the football stadium, the museum offers a pair of solid permanent exhibits (Native American and white settler history), a series of exceptional traveling exhibits (our son particularly enjoyed a look at exotic geckos), and a truly stellar permanent dinosaur exhibit. Originally curated by John R. (Jack) Horner, the museum contains one of the finest collection of Cretaceous-age fossils and associated educational exhibits in the world. After you walk through the dinosaurs, there's a planetarium as well, showing a schedule of short movies throughout the day.

On the face of it, it's perhaps a little odd to consider that the small city of Bozeman should be home to such an impressive museum. But then you think about the role that Montana has played in the history of paleontology.

The Museum of the Rockies in Bozeman, above and left, offers one of the premier dinosaurs exhibits in the world.

The world's first T-rex was found in Montana's Missouri River Breaks in 1902 by Barnum Brown, and Montana State University has a top-shelf paleontology program, producing, over the years, some of the most celebrated paleontologists in the field. Among the various exhibits at the MoR, we particularly appreciate the display of *Triceratops* skulls arranged in escalating age, from infant to adult.

When our little boy was three and four years old, he enjoyed the Yellowstone-themed play area on the third floor. A small handful of interactive exhibits complement the magnetic trout fishing, pretend pup tent, and dress-up area with ranger and fireman costumes.

Summers, the museum also supports an interactive homestead exhibit, a "living history farm," Memorial Day to Labor Day. Volunteers from Bozeman dress in costume and staff the original, 1889 homestead, talking visitors through the daily life of area settlers.

In the summer, the Museum of the Rockies is open daily from 8:00 a.m. to 8:00 p.m. In the winter, they're open from Monday to Saturday, 9:00 a.m. to 5:00 p.m., and Sunday from noon to 5:00 p.m.

Kid Friendly

Between the dinosaurs, the planetarium, the play area, and (during the summer) an interactive outdoor homestead exhibit, we would be hard pressed to think of a more kid-friendly destination in Montana.

EGG MOUNTAIN

EGG MOUNTAIN, ALONG the Rocky Mountain Front south of Choteau, is the site of the world's first discovery of dinosaur embryos. In 1978, a rock-shop owner found a group of small bones that paleontologists Jack Horner and Bob Makela later identified as baby bones belonging to a new species of duck-billed dinosaur. Horner and Makela named the new species *Maiasaura peeblesorum*, or "good mother reptile." The site has since yielded the largest cache of dinosaur eggs, embryos, and baby skeletons in the Western Hemisphere. In addition to *Maiasaura*, a little meat-eating dinosaur named *Troodon* also nested at Egg Mountain. Its eggs indicate that they brooded like birds, with direct contact of the parent. These discoveries led to new ideas about the caretaking capabilities of dinosaurs.

James St. John / CC

48

VISIT THE MONTANA HISTORICAL SOCIETY (ONLINE, FOR NOW)

Established in 1865, the Montana Historical Society is one of the prized institutions in the West.
   Just consider that year for a moment. Eighteen sixty-five. Eleven years before Little Bighorn, twenty-five years before Montana became a state, a few high-minded citizens had the foresight to place a value on our history, even as they were living it. It's the oldest institution of its kind in the American West. Early board members included Wilbur Sanders (who was also, and not necessarily to his credit, involved in the Virginia City vigilante movement), the famous Granville Stuart (Mr. Montana), and Hezekiah L. Hosmer (Chief Justice of the territorial court) as society historian.

A detail from Charles M. Russell and his Friends, *1922, from the Montana Historical Society*

The MHS's collection of artifacts is quite impressive—they have over fifty thousand pieces, and six thousand pieces in the Native American collection alone. That's not to mention the thousand or so pieces in their firearms collection, including Jim Bridger's Hawken rifle and Sitting Bull's Henry repeater. But perhaps most impressive is their art exhibit, which includes more than two hundred pieces from Charles M. Russell as well as some stellar pieces from other American masters.

For a student or a researcher, the MHS is a treasure trove of repository materials not typically shown to the public. The photographic archives have more than five hundred thousand images, and almost every newspaper ever published in Montana is available on microfilm or in digital form. Their manuscript archives include handwritten journals, rare books, papers and photographs relating to C. M. Russell, Teddy

Big Medicine, a rare white buffalo that died in 1959, was once displayed on the second-floor landing of the Historical Society.

"Blue" Abbott, and many others.

The Historical Society is currently moving locations, expanding into a larger, more attractive space that will more than double its current square footage. As of this writing, they are still in the process of that move and are unfortunately closed to visitors. Much of their collection is still available on the Web, however. Go to https://mhs.mt.gov.

Kid Friendly ☆☆☆☆☆

Adults will likely be drawn to the extensive art collection, including the Russell exhibit and some improbable pieces from masters De Kooning and Winold Reiss, among others. Kids will want to spend more time with interpretive historical exhibits and the military collection.

THE BRAY

AFTER YOU GET DONE with the Historical Society, take an hour and walk around the grounds of the Archie Bray Foundation, or the Bray as the locals call it. The exterior is an outdoor art installation. On the west side of Helena, the Bray has been a thing since the 1950s, although its roots go back to 1883. The foundation provides artists residencies, exhibition and sales space, and (perhaps most importantly) they manufacture and sell twenty-some different varieties of clay, with an output of around 700,000 pounds a year. If you have the time, check out their interior exhibition space as well.

A KID'S DAY OUT

Sometimes, you've got to plan an outing just for the kiddos.

Consider starting with a good interactive science museum. For the parents (us), these museums are an opportunity to step back and watch the kids go a little nuts, joyously interact with thoughtful, tactile, stimulating exhibits without too much oversight on our part. For the kids, it's a chance to leave the screens behind and rack up a new experience or two in a safe, controlled environment. As of this writing, our boy is eleven, which feels like the outside edge of what the format really sponsors. He's already a little too cool for school. But for those kids just a hair younger, the science museum is a great way to spend a few hours on an otherwise eventless Saturday.

In Helena, there's ExplorationWorks, two stories of permanent and rotating exhibits. After you're done, there's the carousel next door. There's ice cream, and a movie theater down the way. Burgers and beers at

The Great Northern Carousel in Helena, above and right, has thirty-seven hand-carved animals, as well as an ice-cream counter complete with Montana-made Wilcoxson's ice cream.

ExplorationWorks in Helena, an interactive science museum for kids, is in the Great Northern complex, just west of Last Chance Gulch and just a few steps from the carousel.

the brewhouse for the grownups. It's worth a trip to Helena just to catch the trifecta of science museum, carousel, and Wilcoxson's ice cream, all within a few feet of each other.

In Missoula, there's the spectrUM Discovery Area on Toole Avenue. Combine it with an hour or two at the Dragon Hollow Playground a few blocks away off Front Street or the Silver Summit Playground across the river in McCormick Park.

In Bozeman, try the fantastic Montana Science Center on the west side of town, and in Great Falls, there's the excellent Children's Museum of Montana.

These facilities tend to be operated by passionate volunteers and thoroughly invested professionals. Be polite and courteous, and we doubt they'd say no to a donation.

SKI A MOM-AND-POP DOWNHILL RESORT

Nobody likes a sentence that starts, "Back in my day…"

Nevertheless: Used to be, when we were in high school in the eighties, a season pass to Bridger Bowl was less than a hundred bucks. Pricey but doable. And worth it. Every weekend was a party. A group of cocky sixteen- and seventeen-year-old kids meeting in the lodge, kicking backpacks under the tables, heading up the mountain to spend the morning skiing off Pierre's Knob, Bronco, North Bowl. A few of the more adventurous might hike the Ridge. It was democratic to the extreme. If you could afford to chip in for gas, you could go skiing.

The halcyon days only glow in retrospect. These days, a season pass to Bridger can be over a thousand bucks, the parking spills out toward the highway on weekends, and the lift lines, particularly on the lower mountain, are enough to make you want to bag the whole enterprise. Everybody seems to be in short temper. To the south, a day pass at Big Sky is pushing $225, and the ostentatious displays of wealth make you want to go reactive, full-on redneck. Is any of this something I want to offer to my kids as a model for behavior? Given the barriers to entry (the price of a lift ticket, the crowds, the complicated social context), downhill skiing, while still essential to the Montana experience, isn't quite the slam dunk it used to be.

Great Divide, outside of Helena, offers afternoon skiing by the hour.

Our opinion? Maybe because of those early experiences at Bridger Bowl, the best downhill skiing experiences in Montana are now at the smaller resorts, the Mom-and-Pop places. The skiing can be just

Between Anaconda and Philipsburg, Discovery has fantastic views of Georgetown Lake.

as good, the crowds tend to be less severe, and the social posturing—while not absent—is less obvious. Any hill where folks still ski in Wranglers is all right by us.

By our count, there are at least fifteen ski resorts with lifts in Montana. Eight or ten of these are small enough to offer a good old-fashioned let's-just-go-skiing kind of experience.

Out of Anaconda or Philipsburg, Discovery feels like what Bridger Bowl used to be. Just down the hill from Discovery, Fairmont Hot Springs offers some ski-and-soak combo packages, lift tickets and a couple nights of hotel stay included. We've had problems catching really good snow at Discovery, but the ambiance can't be beat. With expansion and higher prices, bigger crowds from Missoula,

Discovery is edging into resort territory, but hasn't tipped over just yet.

There's Showdown south of Great Falls. There's Red Lodge Mountain and Lost Trail and Maverick and, outside of Helena, there's Great Divide, which still offers afternoon ski passes on an hourly rate.

If you want to save time, rent your skis beforehand from a local ski shop. And before you plan your day, take the time to check out the ski hill's website, verifying the hours and the rates. The smaller places may be closed weekdays, and they may offer limited food service. Plan on packing a lunch just in case.

Kid Friendly

In our experience, kids prefer a simpler, less frenetic, less confusing ski environment. If it takes you longer than ten minutes to walk from the parking lot to the bottom of the first lift, maybe consider another hill.

TICKET PRICES

TICKET PRICES INCREASE every year, of course. As of this writing, these are the maximum adult costs for a day of skiing. Next year, these numbers will be out of date, but they will still show the relative cost between resorts.

Big Sky Resort: $238
Blacktail Mountain: $55
Bridger Bowl: $85
Discovery Ski Area: $65
Great Divide: $64
Lost Trail Ski Area: $58
Maverick Mountain: $45

Montana Snowbowl: $68
Red Lodge Mountain Resort: $101
Showdown: $60
Turner Mountain: $45
Teton Pass Ski Resort: $55
Whitefish Mountain Resort: $89

50

SKI A CLOSED FOREST SERVICE ROAD

Montana's national forests are laced through with an endless, zig-zagging tangle of access roads. Many of these tend to be closed during the winter. You might get a mile or two up a given road but then run into a locked gate. Hopefully there's room for you to turn your truck around.

Each one of these locked gates represents an opportunity. You can still access the road, you just can't use a vehicle. Put the Ford in park, haul out the skis, give the dog a pat, then take off. Go as far up the road as you can, knowing that the return trip, downhill, will be easier.

You'll often share these roads with snowmobilers and snowshoers. Both sets of recreationalists are supposed to respect, as a matter of good form, the established cross-country ski tracks. Don't mind it too much if they don't. Everybody's out here to have a good time.

Carry a backpack with a thermos filled with hot chocolate. Before you turn around, celebrate the end of the road with a mug and a fun-sized Snickers for the kiddos.

Kid Friendly

When it comes to cross-country skiing and kids, the biggest obstacle is finding affordable skis to rent. It's hard to rationalize buying when they're going to grow out of them in five seconds. We've taken to buying but then reselling Online a year later.

51

RENT A SNOWMOBILE

There's a lot to be said for cross-country skiing through a stand of timber on a quiet winter morning. Meditation meets cardio meets a *tiiiny* dollop of self-righteousness. It all makes for one of those luminous days that don't really count against your biblical allotment. Bring a notepad to write down some poetry.

Turn around 180 degrees, however, and there is almost as much to be said for layering up in snowsuits and heavy boots, mittens, a helmet and goggles, firing up a sled that somebody else owns, roaring off through the trees, squinting into a self-generated wind, leaning into the curves, dodging branches, and juking and jiving your way up a mountain. Crows and magpies flare up as you pass.

There seems to be some classist snobbery on the part of both the cross-country folks and the snowmobile folks. If you're a ski enthusiast, it's hard not to resent the riders who tear apart a peaceful winter day with two-stroke crash and clatter. If silence is part of what makes backcountry skiing enjoyable, then their fun largely comes at your expense.

But snowmobilers have their own kind of snobbery. Aggressively embracing their redneckness (for lack of a better word), flaunting their disregard for the quiet.

Kind of like horses and boats, the temptation will be to buy your own snowmobile. Before going down that road, rent first.

Peace. For the cross-country folks, if you haven't tried it, snowmobiling is *fun*, man. So much fun. Try it, then embrace it. Or not. For the snowmobile folks, just try to be courteous. Minimize the disruption if you can.

In Montana, we guess the blue-ribbon snowmobiling destination is maybe West Yellowstone. Cooke City is excellent as well. Seeley Lake is special, as is the national forest south of Big Sky. Anywhere there's room to turn a trailer around in front of a locked Forest Service gate, so long as it's not wilderness or private ground, is fair game. Google snowmobile rentals and call ahead a few weeks in advance. Expect to pay anywhere from $150 to $300 a day, depending on the machine.

Kid Friendly

Your kids will need to be a certain age, but if they're old enough (a moving target, depending on the kiddo), and if they have adequate gear (enough to stay warm), they're going to love snowmobiling.

52

FLY FISH A SPRING CREEK

In the hardcore fly-fishing crowd, Montana is known for its spring creeks. These are streams that maintain consistent water temperatures and flows year-around, and so are more predictable in terms of the quality of their fishing and the size and populations of their trout. As opposed to freestone rivers, which can vary in temperature from just above freezing in the winter to summer highs in the high sixties, spring creeks tend to hover around the low fifties. This steady temperature makes for a friendly environment for the fish, and also allows for consistent hatches of insects. Insect types will vary from season to season, of course, but they can also vary even according to time of day and cloud cover. Regardless, the trout are accustomed to having an insect buffet to choose from, and so they can afford to be choosy in what they take. Spring-creek fishing has been called the graduate school of the fly-fishing world.

Among the most famous are a pair of creeks south of Livingston, both of which flow into the Yellowstone River: Nelson's Spring Creek, on the east side of the Yellowstone, and Armstrong Spring Creek,

Spring-creek fishing in Montana tends to be consistent but difficult. The fish see a lot of flies, and can afford to be choosy.

running through the O'Hair Ranch and the DePuy Ranch, on the west side.

The Nelson family runs Nelson's Spring Creek, and a rod fee will gain you access. You can also stay in overnight cabins that include access to the creek. As of this writing, the Nelsons allow six rods per day on their creek, at a cost of $45 per rod in the winter and $140 per rod at the height of the summer.

Just across the river, Armstrong Spring Creek flows for 1.5 miles, passing through the O'Hair and DePuy properties. Both families offer access. The DePuys charge $80 per rod in the winter and $120 at the height of the summer.

The O'Hairs, upstream from the DePuys, charge the same rates.

We've fished these spring creeks on our own, and we've fished them with guides, and we've always caught three or four times the number of fish with a guide. If you're going to pay the rod fee and make a day of it, you should call one of Livingston's fly shops and try to reserve a qualified guide as well. The families themselves might also be able to recommend someone. As an added incentive, if you're booking for the day, the guide will usually arrange for lunch, and it's almost certainly going to be better than anything that you would have brought.

Kid Friendly

Unless you've got a fly-fishing savant on your hands, spring creek fishing is just too technical for children to enjoy.

RANCH ETIQUETTE

SPENDING ANY TIME AT ALL on a ranch, even just walking through, visitors need to be aware of certain codes of conduct. For starters, if a gate's open, leave it open. If it's closed, you better by god close it again after you're done. Noxious weed dissemination is one of the gravest environmental threats in Montana. There's the Berkeley Pit, then there's knapweed. When you visit a ranch, be sure you've driven your truck through a car wash first. Get the seeds off the wheel wells. If you see trash, pick it up. The rancher's doing you a favor by letting you hunt or fish, so maybe bring some sort of hostess gift when you arrive. Also, say thank you.

FURTHER SUGGESTIONS FOR WINTER

Go Ice Skating

Every largeish Montana community maintains some sort of ice skating rink in the winter. A good portion also offer equipment rentals. Don't forget the helmets.

Tie a Fly

If you like fly fishing, eventually you will try to tie your own flies. Do it this winter, if only because it will give you the chance to daydream about where you're going to be fishing in a few short months.

Find an Unexpected Book

When it comes to libraries, Montana's got it made. Bozeman, Missoula, and Billings both have top-shelf, newer facilities. On a gray, snowy afternoon, libraries are warm and always welcoming.

Go Dog Sledding

Winter resorts often offer dog sled trips as amenities. Google dog sledding in your area, then make the reservation. Why not?

ACKNOWLEDGMENTS

Pretty much any guidebook is going to be reliant on those books and magazines that have preceded it. We would like to acknowledge our debt to the shelf full of titles that have helped steer us through the state.

Falcon Guides have been around since the late seventies or early eighties, when a literary entrepreneur in Helena started up the business. Not quite so homegrown as they used to be (they've since been acquired at least twice by out of state companies), these guidebooks have nevertheless been the bedrock on which so much else has been built. Look for the gold and black covers.

Based in Helena, Farcountry Press *is* still homegrown, however, and has contributed any number of important titles to help bring context and dimension to your Montana experience.

Riverbend Press, also based in Helena, and Mountain Press in Missoula both continue to produce beautiful, top-shelf reference materials.

Finally, and most importantly, a number of the items in this guidebook have also been mentioned by *Montana Outdoors* in their two special issues, "Best 100" and "Next 100." They'll take up where this book leaves off. Go to https://fwp.mt.gov/montana-outdoors/best-100 for more information. You should probably subscribe while you're there.

www.ingramcontent.com/pod-product-compliance
Lightning Source LLC
Chambersburg PA
CBHW042134160426
43199CB00022B/2910